Activate

An Entirely New Approach
to Small Groups

Nelson Searcy
and **Kerrick Thomas**

Regal

From Gospel Light
Ventura, California, U.S.A.

Published by Regal
From Gospel Light
Ventura, California, U.S.A.
www.regalbooks.com
Printed in the U.S.A.

Library of Congress Cataloging-in-Publication Data
Searcy, Nelson.
  Activate : an entirely new approach to small groups / Nelson Searcy and Kerrick Thomas.
    p. cm.
  ISBN 978-0-8307-4566-1 (trade paper)
  1. Church group work. 2. Small groups. I. Thomas, Kerrick. II. Title.
  BV652.2.S43 2008
  253'.7—dc22

                                                                        2008003484

Rights for publishing this book outside the U.S.A. or in non-English languages are administered by Gospel Light Worldwide, an international not-for-profit ministry. For additional information, please visit www.glww.org, email info@glww.org, or write to Gospel Light Worldwide, 1957 Eastman Avenue, Ventura, CA 93003, U.S.A.

Contents

We haven't always loved the idea of small groups. In fact, as recently as six years ago, we didn't think very highly of small groups at all. Maybe you feel this way too. And maybe, like us, you know that small groups are part of God's plan for spiritual maturity . . . but you can see that current small-group systems simply aren't working. Perhaps you are asking yourself the same questions we asked in the beginning of our small groups journey. Questions such as:

- Is it possible to have a small groups ministry at my church that isn't complicated?
- Is it possible to operate a small groups ministry without hiring dozens of staff people?
- Is it possible to see 100 percent adult attender participation in groups?
- Is it possible for true life-change to happen in groups?
- Is it possible to have a small groups ministry that my staff and I are passionate about?

In this book, we will walk you down our path of conversion from being apathetic toward small groups to becoming raving fans of small groups. We believe that we have found a way for groups to be simple, self-sustaining and life changing. Our change of heart didn't happen overnight. Rather, it took place little by little, through the life of our local church: The Journey Church in New York City.

Our small groups system is a ministry first. But beyond that, it is a simple, reproducible process that you can use year in and year out to see God-honoring results. We strongly believe that while the scriptural small-group idea is right, much of the recent small groups thinking has been wrong. When it comes to implementing effective groups, there's a system problem, not a scriptural problem. Too many churches' small groups systems make false assumptions about groups. One of our goals over the last few years has been to challenge current, widely held assumptions and find a system that keeps the New Testament integrity of small groups while accomplishing New Testament results (all of which we will define in the book).

We have found a system that works. Our heart is to teach you how to implement this system in your church in a way that will change lives and bring God glory. Having run this system for many years at our church, and coached hundreds of church leaders and intensely trained numbers of churches, we can state with assurance that this small groups system is possible in churches from New York City to New Mexico. And it is possible in your church!

Here are some guidelines for achieving your small groups goals in your church.

1. *Read and digest this book.* Grab a highlighter and work your way through the following pages. Make notes in the margins, disagree with us, laugh at us or raise your eyebrows. We don't mind. Over the next 200 pages, we are going to show you a small groups system that can consistently accomplish the goals we mentioned above.

2. *Study this book with others on your staff or in your church.* Any successful small groups ministry or system will require the commitment of dozens, if not hundreds, of people. This book is designed for local church discussion.

3. *Be open to new ideas.* Our small groups system is contrarian. It goes against some of the current small groups theories, and there may be times when you are taken aback or get

angry with us. That's okay. Don't let discomfort close your mind. We are not being contrarian for contrarian's sake (like, say, Andy Rooney). Our thinking is the result of a lot of trial and error, flights and crashes, and some God-sized successes that surprised even us. The ideas presented here were not discovered easily or cheaply, but through working day in and day out with the group members and group leaders at our church, and with hundreds of other church leaders around the nation. Our contrarian ideas challenge modern theories, not Scripture essentials, so please keep an open mind.

The goal of this book is to help you develop a small groups system that both you and your people can be excited about, and that can help you realize God's dream for your unique church. We have been praying for you as we've written what you are about to read and can't wait to see what God does through your willingness to step out of your comfort zone and *activate*!

PART ONE

The Activate Mindset

Rethinking Small-Group Methodology

Big Idea #1: Think from the Inside Out . . . Not from the Outside In

Conventional Wisdom: *Take care of those on the inside first.*

Reality: *Small groups that focus on serving their own members rather than on reaching out to others quickly become inwardly focused and stagnant.*

Have you ever experienced a paradigm shift? If so, you know the power it has to revolutionize your way of thinking. The actual term "paradigm shift" first made its way onto our culture's radar when Thomas Kuhn wrote his enlightening book *The Structure of Scientific Revolutions* in the early sixties. Through his research, Kuhn proved that practically every worthwhile discovery or breakthrough is the result of a release from a tradition or an old way of thinking. Commenting on the power of Kuhn's observations on this topic, Stephen Covey wrote, "Paradigm shifts move us from one way of seeing the world to another. And those shifts can create powerful change. Our paradigms, whether correct or incorrect, are the sources of our attitudes and behaviors."[1] Every one of the ideas that we are going to present to you in the next 12 chapters will likely shift some of your paradigms, but probably none more greatly than the idea we begin with here: *Think from the outside in, not from the inside out.*

Human nature and decades of church tradition have taught us that small study gatherings, whether they are actual small groups or some variant of Sunday School, are about getting our congregation to interact on a more intimate level. These groups are obviously focused directly on the people who are most involved in your church, right? Those are *your people*. That's who you need to get to sign up. Then, once in the group, you teach them and take care of their needs. Well, of course that makes sense on the surface, but when we look a little deeper, this kind of mindset signals what we call "inward" thinking. And when a church starts or restructures a small groups system with an inward mindset, guess what happens? Their overall growth, both numerical and spiritual, stagnates or declines. Something's not right.

Ask the Right Question

When church leaders set up their small groups system with the committed people of their church in mind, they inevitably create a process that makes it easy for members and regular attenders to get signed up, or signed up again, as the case may be. But what about those people who are new to the church, have never been in a small group or who only come occasionally? If you want to grow your small groups and your church, you have to intentionally target those who are not yet in the system.

Wrong Question: How do I get people to sign up again?

Right Question: How do I get new people to sign up?

The paradox is this: If you focus on getting new people to sign up for a group, you will get both new sign-ups and re-sign-ups. If you focus only on re-sign-ups, you only get re-sign-ups.

In *The Purpose Driven Church*, Rick Warren introduced the Circles of Commitment. The concept, which applies directly to small groups, is that the goal of your church is to move people from the outer circle (low commitment/maturity) to the inner circle (high commitment/ maturity). Each of the circles represents a different level of development and involvement:

As leaders, our ultimate purpose and overarching responsibility is to move people from the Community to the Core as they come to know God and learn to be fully developing followers of Jesus. But sometimes in ministry—especially when it comes to small groups—we get caught up around the Congregation level and forget about the people who comprise our Crowd and the greater Community.

We all know that evangelism moves people from the Community to the Crowd, and traditional thinking says that the primary purpose of small groups is to move people from the Congregation to the Committed and from the Committed to the Core. Small groups do play a role in doing that. But what if we were to tell you that the most powerful potential for your small groups lies in their ability to move people from the Crowd to the Congregation? What if we were to tell you that your small groups system should be designed first and foremost for those who are not yet involved in them—those who are not yet assimilated?

If your focus is primarily on serving your Congregation with groups and not on connecting the people who make up your Crowd, your momentum will turn inward and your growth will stop. To make sure you aren't falling into this trap, continually be asking yourself, "What are the needs of those not in groups? How do I set up this system so that it focuses on getting new people to sign up?" Keep your thinking in the two outer circles. If you don't continually check the pulse on this issue, you are going to miss out on some fruit.

Big Number vs. Little Number

So how do you know who is in your Crowd? Is your Congregation really what you think it is? What would you think if we could show you how your attendance number may actually be much higher than you realize? You'd probably be pretty skeptical at first. Of course you know your attendance number, right? Probably not. Get ready for a paradigm shift. When it comes to your attendance, you actually have two numbers that are crucial for you to consider—your Big Number and your Little Number. Without getting too technical, let us explain:

Little Number
Your Little Number is the average number of people attending on a Sunday (measured over a three-month period). This is your weekly attendance, or your "Congregation." Contrary to popular belief, this *is not the number* you work with when you start planning your small groups. Most people make the mistake of saying, "Okay, I have X number of people every Sunday, so how do I get them in small groups?" That is wrong thinking.

Big Number
Your Big Number is the number of individual people who have attended your church over that same three-month period. That's your "Crowd." Think about it: Not everyone who calls your church his or her home church shows up every week. Each Sunday, your congregation is a mix of different people. But if you took all of those people that have shown

up at least once in the last three months and put them in a room together, how many people would there be?

If your church averages about 80 people on a Sunday, you probably
have 100 to 125 individual people coming through your doors over the
course of three months and calling your church "home." If you average
1,400, you may have as many as 3,000 in your Crowd. The key to building healthy, thriving small groups is to create a system that targets your
Big Number. Ask yourself, "How can I get as many of my Crowd into
small groups as possible?" Your Congregation is included in that effort,
by default, but does not limit it. And as you focus your small-group sign-
ups in a way that pulls as many members of the Crowd in as possible,
you set up their assimilation into the Congregation (for more on the
Assimilation process, see *Fusion: Turning First-Time Guests to Fully Engaged
Members*). Small groups close the back door for those people who like
the breeze a little too much. If you learn to target your Big Number as
you build and implement small groups, you can consistently have more
than 100 percent of your average Sunday attendance in groups.

Knowing your Big Number changes the way you do things. Your focus becomes that larger group that you never realized was truly a part of
your church. There is no rule of thumb for figuring out exactly what
your Big Number is. It's affected by things such as the age of the church,
its influence in the community, and whether there have been any moral
failures or issues that have caused division. Make an educated guess and
then focus your energies on that number. Small groups really do move
people along the continuum from the Crowd to the Congregation and
then inside the circle to the Committed and the Core, if they are correctly focused. As those in your Crowd create relationships with others
and take on the responsibilities that come with being in a group, they
will go from being sporadic and occasional attenders to regular attenders who are involved, committed, serving and growing. But they will
only be part of your small groups system if you shift that old paradigm
and make it a point to start thinking from the outside in!

Big Idea #2: Think Larger . . . Not Smaller

Conventional Wisdom: *Smaller groups lead to increased intimacy, deeper relationships and more significant spiritual growth.*

Reality: *Groups with 7 members or fewer are difficult to lead and more likely to fail, which means they have little to no chance of fostering healthy relationships or spiritual growth, while groups of 12 to 15 people do both more effectively.*

While conventional wisdom teaches that smaller groups of people are better at cultivating deep relationships and discovering spiritual truths together, that's just not the case. Of course, it sounds good, right? Small group gurus like to tell us that if too many people are in a group, it will lose its sense of intimacy. They say that people will become frustrated because they won't be able to be heard, and meaningful relationships will be hard to establish. In theory, you may agree. But here's the problem: In practice, smaller groups simply aren't as effective as larger groups. We've discovered time and time again that most people:

- feel more comfortable in larger groups
- are more likely to sign up for larger groups
- stay plugged in longer in larger groups
- form deeper connections and grow spiritually in larger groups

The majority of churches doing small groups fall into the conventional trap, at some point, of thinking smaller is better. As a result, they try to limit each of their groups to about 7 people. That is a big mistake. Why?

1. Not Everyone Who Signs Up Shows Up
Not everyone who signs up for a group is going to show up every week. Let's play this out: Say you cap your groups at 7 sign-ups. At least 1 of

the people who signed up will never show up for the group. You can also be assured that at least 1 to 2 people will have to miss the group almost every week, because of something like a scheduling conflict or an illness. So you are already down 3 people each week. Realistically, you are looking at only having 4 to 5 people in the room, because you only allowed 7 to sign up. And if that group of 4 to 5 includes people who don't participate readily or don't get along well with each other, the leader is in real trouble. However, if you let 15 to 20 people sign up for each group, and the same scenario plays itself out, you will still have at least 10 people at every meeting, which eases a lot of pressure and facilitates real growth.

2. Fewer People Means More Work

When groups are extremely small, the group leader has to be more skilled and has to work harder to make the group a success. In such groups, the leader often has to take on the role of a teacher instead of facilitator, especially during the first few weeks of group meetings when members may be hesitant to speak up.

Even if everyone does speak, there are so few people that the conversation will be harder to keep alive. So the leader has to prepare much more diligently and be ready to carry the full weight of the discussion. This fact alone will limit your number of potential group leaders and cripple the growth of your system.

But in a larger group, the leader can count on more group members participating in the discussion. There will almost always be someone with something to say. When more people are involved, the leader's job is less stressful and more fun, which leads to better groups and fewer burned-out leaders. You always want people to leave the weekly meeting wanting more. It's better to have time run out with things still in full swing than for the discussion to dry up in the first 15 minutes, leaving people awkwardly looking at their watches and thinking up excuses for why they won't be able to return the next week.

3. You Need to Minimize the "Weirdo" Factor

Many new believers and new attenders don't sign up for a small group because they are afraid they will end up with people they consider strange. Deep down, hesitant members are asking themselves, *If these people are all weirdoes, what will I do? How will I get out?!* In the name of political correctness, we wish we could dismiss this fear completely, but all church leaders know that it's a reality. Sometimes individuals sign up who make the group uncomfortable for everyone. With 7 or fewer members, there is a much greater risk that the group will be negatively affected by someone who makes things awkward. Similarly, new and prospective group members are also afraid that if the group is really small, they may not click with anyone at all.

You can eliminate such fears by allowing more people to sign up, where chances are better that everyone will be able to relate to and connect with at least a few people. And even if there is a "weirdo" in the group, his or her impact will be greatly lessened. The sheer number of other people will help buffer the distraction. Also, a larger group allows hesitant members to stay a little anonymous at first until they find their place and identify the people who they feel most comfortable connecting with. By taking the pressure off, you open the door for more people to be eager to get involved.

Bigger Is Better

In our experience, groups of seven or fewer people have a significantly higher failure rate, produce less fruit and cause the leader more frustration and anxiety than larger groups. That's why if one of our small groups has fewer than eight people signed up we classify it as being in the "Danger Zone." The most common reason group leaders give for not wanting to lead again is that they did not have a good experience in their last group, usually because it was too small. We often survey small-group members at the end of a semester. Those who give groups less than excellent scores almost always comment that their group was small and therefore strained. They say that they did not get to meet as many new people as they had wanted to and that the group's interaction and discussions were uncomfortable. So, what's the solution? Bigger groups. Here are two important steps to make sure that you are *thinking larger*:

1. Allow Up to 20 People to Sign up for Each of Your Groups

By allowing this many people to sign up, your projected number of *actual attendees* on a weekly basis will be 12 to 15. When the weekly attendance falls within that range, the group is structured for success and the members of the group will be likely to report a great experience. This may mean having fewer groups overall, but in the end, having more people signed up in fewer groups that are structured for success is a better way to go.

2. Consider Groups with Fewer than 8 People in the Danger Zone

If you have less than 8 people signed up, your group is in the Danger Zone. Don't cancel the group, but be aware that this group has greater potential to run into trouble. Here are some action steps for groups in the Danger Zone:

- Leave sign-ups open longer than usual—even after the group has started meeting.

- Provide weekly encouragement and guidance for the leaders of these groups. They will be feeling anxious and frustrated. If you don't help them through, they probably won't step up to lead again.

- Evaluate why so few people are signing up. Is there an issue with the leader? Is the topic or study that was chosen unpopular for some reason? Perhaps the time and location is not convenient for many people. We have had to make changes to groups at the last minute because of all these issues. Don't be afraid to make the necessary adjustments.

Thinking larger rather than smaller is one of the most helpful Big Ideas for group leaders. Next to implementing the semester-based start and stop times, which we will discuss later, making this shift to slightly bigger groups will increase the loyalty and effectiveness of your group leaders tenfold. While church leaders are often a little hesitant to make the shift, our experience has shown that group leaders love the results. They relish the strong interaction that takes place in larger groups versus the tension and hard work that generally come with trying to lead smaller groups. Remember, bigger is better. Give your small-group members and your leaders the best opportunity for success by thinking larger, not smaller!

Big Idea #3: Think Friends . . . Not Intimacy

Conventional Wisdom: *Small groups are a place where intimate relationships are formed.*

Reality: *Small groups are a place where new friendships are formed.*

Have you ever had to deal with the pink elephant in the room? Or the 800-pound gorilla? You know, the thing that everyone knows is there but no one wants to acknowledge?

We've come to think of Big Idea #3 as the pink elephant in the room of small groups planning. We all know, deep down, that it is true, but it is so ingrained in conventional small groups wisdom that no one wants to acknowledge it. After all, if it's said out loud, groups as we know them might cease to exist. Well, the time has come. We are going to step out on a limb here and give voice to the truth we've all been avoiding: *Small groups are not the best place for intimate relationships to form.* There. The elephant and the gorilla may now make their exits as we explore this seemingly blasphemous comment.

On one level or another, we've all bought into the widely accepted theory that small groups are a place where participants can get deeply personal with one another and find lifelong friends. This thinking is what leads most churches to set up a small groups structure where individual groups meet anywhere from 18 months to the Second Coming of Jesus. The groups need *time*, they argue, for members to truly bond and become intimately involved in each other's lives. Their goal is to nurture soul-baring relationships.

Unfortunately, this mindset doesn't just show up in back-end planning. Most churches go so far as to promise their attenders that they will find meaningful, intimate relationships with fellow Christians if they join a group. But if we step back and take an honest look at what actually goes on in healthy small groups, we have to admit that this isn't what happens at all. Too often, we find the exact opposite. In the end, promises of close friendship at the outset lead to less spiritual growth, more frustration and fewer people signing up for your church's small groups.

Small groups are not the place for your people to form intimate, meaningful relationships with one another. Instead, they are a place to form new, basic friendships. It's important for us to make another point here that, while controversial, we feel is also quite freeing. In saying that small groups are a place for friendships and not intimacy, we are not lowering the bar for our small groups in any way. When it comes to spiritual formation, both friendship and intimacy are necessary in helping us become more like Jesus. Small groups are most effective for helping people make godly friends, not for helping them form intimate relationships within the context of the group. They may ultimately form intimate relationships with people they've met in a group, but that will happen outside of the system.

The Four Spaces of Spiritual Growth

Even the sheer psychology of small-group dynamics supports the fact that, conventionally, we have been trying to force a level of familiarity in an environment that's not conducive to it. In his book *The Search to Belong*, Joseph Myers points out that there are four physical spaces where we exist and live in relationship with other people.[2] These are also the four spaces where we grow spiritually. Here is a quick overview of the Four Spaces of Spiritual Growth.

1. Public Space

The first space in which people can experience growth is a public space. Such a space is defined as a group of 20 or more people, where there is usually about 12 feet between each person. Even when people are closer than 12 feet from each other, there is little to no personal interaction. People don't know the names of those around them. In a learning environment, which is a common public space, there is usually a teacher or lecturer who serves as the focal point and communicates to the group as a whole. *Examples of public spaces include church, the mall, a concert or a sporting event.*

2. Social Space

People can also grow in a social space, which consists of a gathering of anywhere from 5 to 20 people. The people in this group are usually 4 to 12 feet from one another. Everyone in a social space will know your name though they won't know your personal business. In a social space you don't need a lecturer or teacher, but you do need a leader or facilitator if you want to focus the attention of the group in one direction or encourage a common group discussion. A social space is the most conducive environment for getting to know new people. *Examples of social spaces include the break room at work or school, a fun event at church, or just hanging out with some buddies somewhere.*

3. Personal Space

In a personal space there are usually 2 to 5 people present. The space between people is anywhere from 18 inches to 4 feet. Everyone in your personal space will know more than just your name; they will know details about your life. Our personal spaces are usually filled with friends and peers. No leader, facilitator or teacher is necessary. Personal space is private space. Outsiders are not welcome. *Examples of personal space include best friends on a park bench, road trips, small coffee tables and personal conversation that you wouldn't want just anyone to hear.*

4. Intimate Space

In an intimate space there is only one other person present. The space between the two individuals is less than 18 inches. People in your intimate space know more than your business—they know your secrets. They know you better than anyone else in the world. Where personal space involves good friends, intimate space involves someone you consider "family." *Examples of intimate space include romantic destinations, private dinners, any space geared toward personal communication.*

Five Truths About the Four Spaces

Here are a few truths about the Four Spaces of Spiritual Growth.

1. We Grow Spiritually and Connect with Others in All Four Spaces

For example, the public space is the least intimate space, but who could deny that we grow spiritually in significant ways through the teaching of God's Word at church? And who could deny that a sense of identification and connectedness forms with the larger group during worship? All four spaces—even the least intimate—have tremendous value for our spiritual growth and relationships.

2. We Need Relationships in All Four Spaces

The goal is not to have balance in all four spaces but to have harmony between the spaces. For instance, we will naturally have more people in our social space than in our intimate space, and that's as it should be. The key is to have people in all four spaces. We are not healthy relationally if we are lacking connections in one or more of the spaces.

3. No One Space Is More Important than the Others

We need all four to grow and to be spiritually healthy. Consider which is worse: Someone locked away in a cabin with only one person to talk to (even if that person is an intimate relationship), or someone who is always around a crowd of people but has no friends or family to share intimately with? Both are equally unhealthy, because God created us to need various kinds of relationships to survive and grow.

4. The Spaces Are Interrelated and Connected Together

For instance, public spaces give us the opportunity to identify those people we'll invite into our social space. In the social space, we identify our closest friends with whom we'll spend time in the personal space. And in either our social space or our personal space, we'll find those special relationships that become intimate.

5. We Have a Deficit of Social Space

Americans today have a deficit of social space. Of course, we don't see this problem in high school and college. During those years, ready-made social spaces are all around us. But after graduation, we have a hard time finding safe social spaces where we can meet together with 5 to 20 peers. The front porch (or the front stoop in New York City) used to be the primary place to socialize in American society. But increasingly today, Americans value privacy, safety and convenience and stay locked behind many layers of security in their homes, impenetrable to neighbors or passersby.

Unfortunately, there are some devastating relational consequences to this breakdown in the traditional American social space.

First, as a result of the breakdown in our social relationships, we experience a breakdown in our personal and intimate relationships. As mentioned, our personal and intimate relationships (outside of immediate family) come directly from our social relationships. When there are no social relationships, there is no pool to draw from to find a best friend or an intimate relationship.

Second, because there are fewer safe places to socialize, we look to unsafe places to find those personal and intimate relationships we need. That is part of the reason why we have seen the rise in Internet chat rooms, speed dating and hanging out in bars. People will settle for unhealthy relationships rather than have no relationships at all.

So what does this have to do with small groups in your church?

Activate Principle
Allow casual friendships to develop without feeling a need to force intimacy.

Most of the people in your church are looking for social relationships. They want to meet casual friends—people who will be their "buddies." They are looking for people to hang out with, because they know that from that group of people they'll be able to identify those they want to get personal with and invite into their inner circle. Then, from that inner circle, they can decide who they want to be in intimate relationship with. They don't want to be forced into contrived familiarity. They simply want to be given an opportunity to connect with new people so that relationships can develop naturally.

For most of us, our mistake in this area of small groups has been twofold. First, we have *undersold* the importance of basic friendships and social relationships to overall spiritual health. Second, we have *oversold* the importance of personal and intimate relationships and have tried to force our small-group members into such relationships, even though our small groups have always been fundamentally structured to accommodate social, not personal or intimate, connections. People do not get personal or intimate in groups of 8 to 15 people. We socialize in groups of 8 to 15 people. Social relationships form best in groups. When we try to force intimate relationships in our groups, we scare and alienate many potential group members, especially men. No man is going to sign up for a group if he thinks he is going to have to let people in a social space into his personal business. But men (and women) will sign up for groups where they can meet new friends, connect with God and hang out socially. And from that group, both men and women will successfully identify the people they want to allow into their personal and intimate space. And get this: Those personal and intimate relationships will form and develop naturally outside of the group.

When we try to induce intimacy, not only do we make it so that people are hesitant to join, but we also set up our group leaders for failure. If we set a goal in front of our leaders to get people to enter personal and/or intimate relationships, then they feel like they didn't do their job if everyone in the group doesn't bond and become best friends. Intimacy cannot be forced. It's a work of the Holy Spirit. And we can absolutely guarantee this: In a group larger than five, it is impossible for every person to become intimate or even personal, even if you try to force the group to stay together for years. Odds are that some people just aren't going to mesh.

Activate Principle
Groups help us form personal and intimate relationships by providing a safe space within the group where we make friends who could then become more intimate friends outside of the group.

Reshaping Small Groups as Places to Meet Friends

So what does this mean for small groups? In light of these realities, how should our small groups function? The answer is simple: Groups should be a safe, comfortable, stress-free place where individuals have the opportunity to meet new people, make new friends, learn something new and grow spiritually within a social context. Here are three steps you can take to make sure your small groups are structured for success:

1. *Have specific beginning and ending dates for your small groups.* Small groups at The Journey generally last from 10 to 12 weeks. This gives people the freedom and flexibility to make a commitment they know they can stick with. Then, if a few people connect and become good friends, they can choose to be in a group together the next semester as well. Inevitably, they'll also continue to develop their relationships and accountability outside of the group. But if the people in the group do not hit it off with one another, they are not forced to stay together past the end date of the group.

2. *Let your group leaders know what a group "win" is.* Your leaders are not supposed to make everyone in the group best friends, and they don't need to feel any pressure to do so. Don't let them think that if everyone isn't crying together, sharing intimate details of their lives or getting together outside of the group that they have failed. They haven't. We make sure our group leaders understand that their small group "wins" when, throughout the semester, the Bible is applied in a practical way to the lives of those in the group and everyone in the group prays together. That's it! That's all! As a result, nearly all of our groups are successful.

3. *Promote your groups as a social space—a safe place to meet new people, make friends, grow in faith and have fun.* Don't promise meaningful or life-changing relationships. First of all, if you promise personal and intimate relationships and they are not delivered, people may leave the group feeling like it was a failure and not want to join again. At the end of the group, most people will feel like their group was a failure. Second, most people don't want to sign up for a mushy "share everything" kind of group (especially men). Promote your groups as a social space and watch your small-group sign-ups soar!

Remember that you cannot engineer or force relationships in your groups. That's not your job. That's the work of the Holy Spirit. And it's not what your people really want, anyway. Your prospective small-group members are looking for a social space where they can meet new friends. As you discover how to effectively create that environment, the personal and intimate relationships you want your people to develop will happen naturally. No, it's not conventional. But then again, neither is God!

Notes

1. Stephen R. Covey, *The 7 Habits of Highly Effective People* (New York: Free Press, 2004), p. 29.
2. Joseph Myers, *The Search to Belong: Rethinking Intimacy, Community and Small Groups* (Grand Rapids, MI: Zondervan, 2003).

Rethinking Small-Group Structure

Big Idea #4: Think Short-Term . . .
Not Long-Term

Conventional Wisdom: *Small groups should last anywhere from 18 months to eternity*

Reality: *The ideal length for a small group is 10 to 12 weeks.*

When you realize that the goal of your small groups is not to catalyze intimate relationships, you find the freedom to structure them more effectively. You can start asking questions such as, *What structure is going to best promote spiritual growth?* and *What structure will encourage the greatest number of people to sign up?* When we began asking ourselves these questions early on in the development of The Journey's small groups system, the answers were clear. The same type of system we had all been in for most of our lives would also work best for small groups. That is, a semester-based system, modeled after the ubiquitous American educational calendar.

Philosophy 101

Do you ever have the urge to buy school supplies in early September? Don't you feel like the world winds down to a slow crawl around Christmas and New Year's? Do you find yourself eager for a fresh start when spring arrives? Because we have all grown up in the modern educational system, we are wired to associate feelings of new beginnings and natural endings with certain times of the year. There is a natural flow in how we relate to the progression of our months. This truth played a major role in the development of The Journey's semester-based small-group philosophy. We already knew that short-term groups were more effective than long-term groups (as we'll prove), but we weren't sure how to structure them. So we decided that, instead of trying to work against what is built into our attenders' DNA, we would take advantage of it.

Think about it. In the first 400 years of Christianity, the gospel spread more quickly than at any other time in history. Why? Because there was a cultural infrastructure in place that the church was wise enough to take advantage of. Early church leaders used the natural systems of society and cultural thought to carry the good news about Jesus to the world. Logistically speaking, they worked with what people knew and accepted as normal—such as the *Koine* Greek language, the Roman road system and the existing holiday structure—rather than force them to fit into an unnatural mold in order be a part of the church.

Unfortunately, in the modern church, we have separated ourselves so far from society that we have essentially created an alternate mode of existence. And when someone comes through our doors, we ask them to take sides. We give the impression that if you are going to be a Christian, you have to go to a Christian school, listen only to Christian music, shop at Christian stores, go to Christian movies and eat Christian candy bars. Instead of using the natural infrastructures of society to spread the gospel, we have developed our own competing system. As we have insisted that people do things the "Christian" way, even if it makes no sense to how they are wired by God to operate, we have limited our ability to share the truth effectively. We have stood by our own structure to the detriment of our mission.

At The Journey, taking a cue from the early gospel spreaders, we began asking ourselves, *What can we adapt from culture that would give momentum and success to our small groups system?* The answer was immediately clear. Our culture is defined by its education. People adhere to the flow of the educational system throughout their developmental years. As grown-ups, that doesn't change. Either our lives still revolve around the academic calendar because we have kids in school, or we are likely involved in some form of continuing education ourselves. Even the farthest removed adult still feels like he or she should get a summer vacation. We know and inherently respond to the structure of this system. So, if we look a little deeper, we also understand that the educational system has something figured out. They know that we grow best through the built-in "stress and release" periods that make up the school year. That is, we grow most effectively in a semester-based system.

Semesters are, by definition, time-bound. In studying small groups systems around the country and developing our own, we have discovered that time-bound groups are the best way to foster and maintain spiritual growth. While most small groups philosophies will tell you that groups need to last anywhere from 18 months until death-do-us-part, we believe that 10 to 12 weeks is the perfect length for a healthy group. When you put time-bound groups in place, and mold them around the natural flow of the academic year, you encourage more people to sign up and you guard against the very real danger of stagnation.

Encourage Sign-Ups

Getting people to sign up for small groups is an ongoing stressor for many churches, but it doesn't have to be. Putting time boundaries on groups will facilitate more eager sign-ups and take pressure off of the system. So often, in our separate Christian bubble, we ask people to do things they would never be comfortable doing in other areas of their lives. For instance, we ask them to sign up for groups that have no definite end date. Can you imagine if you wanted to take a personal-growth seminar at a community center but you couldn't pin down any information on when it would be over? You probably wouldn't go. Or imagine if you wanted to take a course at a local college starting in the fall, but no one could tell you when the term would end. In fact, they seemed to think it might go on indefinitely. Makes no sense, right? But that's exactly what most churches are doing with small groups. So many of us are asking people to commit to something that has no end in sight. That's intimidating, unnatural and unrealistic. And the truth is, most men won't do it.

Early on, we learned that it is much easier to get women connected with a small group than it is to get men connected. So, we decided that if we focused on what it would take to get men to join, those efforts would definitely be enough to make sure the women were on board as well. One thing we know about men is that most of them (including both of us), in the beginning especially, are already skeptical about joining a small group. They don't like the idea of being put in a room with people they don't know. They don't like the idea of sharing their feelings. They consider themselves to be extremely busy. You cannot ask or expect them to willingly make a commitment to an unending group. Sure, you will get some men to join, but you will inevitably turn off even more. People want a specific beginning date and a specific ending date.

Good thing for us that such predetermined periods are also an important key for maximizing spiritual growth. We need periods of stress followed by periods of release in order to reach our potential in any area.

Activate Principle

People grow over short periods of time (stress). Then they need to rest (release). After the period of rest, they can grow again (stress) . . . and the growth cycle continues.

We understand the principle of stress and release in other areas of our lives. I (Nelson) have two brothers who are bodybuilders. From them

I have learned the science of bodybuilding. (It's a science I choose not to apply, but that's another story.) In bodybuilding, the key is to stress a specific muscle group one day and then let it rest the next. While logic may suggest that continual stress on the muscles would cause them to grow, it actually causes deterioration. Growth happens during the rest period. Without rest, the muscles can't build themselves up.

Even God mandated a rest period—the Sabbath. Psychological studies have confirmed God's warning that working without a day of rest leads to fatigue, corrosion, burnout and breakdown. God put the stress-and-release principle in place by establishing six days for work followed by a day for rest. The same principle is crucial for small groups systems.

When people are "stressed" and then "released," they grow much deeper in their spiritual walk and much closer to other believers than when the stress period continues indefinitely. In the semester-based system, groups last for approximately three months. At the end of that three-month semester, there is a month to six weeks where groups are not meeting. Then the new semester begins and everyone is in groups again for three months. Then another break. When small-group attenders are in a system that is based on this process, they grow closer to God, grow deeper in their relationships with other people, are more likely to serve, and become more committed to the church than people who attend a group every week indefinitely. By adhering to their natural need to take breaks and "rest," they go further and faster than they would otherwise.

Life, and small groups, is a series of sprints (not a marathon) followed by a time of rest to catch your breath and prepare for the next sprint. This growth cycle is wired into our DNA. Spiritual growth flourishes in periods of concentrated immersion followed by periods of reflection. Intimacy with others comes from being around them, then being away from them. The down time allows for growth. Our small groups will be more effective if we lay their foundation on top of the way God created us, rather than trying to institute our own regimens.

Seven Advantages of Time-Bound Groups

1. A clear beginning and end date
2. Easier for people to make short-term commitments
3. Allows time for groups promotion and sign-ups
4. Easier for people to get into a group when everyone is starting at the same time
5. More group options—new topics offered each semester
6. Matches the academic calendar year
7. Allows for the growth that comes through a stress-and-release cycle

Stopping Stagnation

Molding your small-group calendar into a semester-based system will also help you guard against stagnation. When you have a group that goes on and on, two things will inevitably begin to happen: (1) Group leaders will burn out, and (2) group members will get too comfortable. God doesn't grow us when we are comfortable. We have found that if a small group of people is not growing, it's because no new elements have been introduced into the group recently. As soon as a new element is introduced, the group will start to grow. That goes for community groups, recovery groups and your small groups.

Activate Principle

I don't grow if I'm not stepping out of my comfort zone and exposing myself to new people and new ideas.

We get comfortable with each other pretty quickly. In small groups, when people start getting so comfortable with each other that they know what other group members are going to say before they say it, growth stagnates. Think about another parallel with the athletic word: physical fitness. To get into physical shape requires going beyond our comfort zone and persisting through discomfort. The old saying is true: no pain, no gain. Spiritual growth does not happen when we are constantly living within our comfort zone. When we are in the same group with the same people month after month, we get too comfortable and stagnate.

Stagnation usually happens if a group is together for longer than 16 to 18 weeks. Sometimes you will get a group that wants to stay together from one semester to the next. That's fine, as long as you open the groups up at the end of the semester, allowing new people to join (or re-join) and others to leave. When you reopen the groups, there is a natural break. People will inevitably see a new group that interests them or decide to lead a group themselves, and things will shift. Even in those groups where the members are "determined" to stay together, things will change. You don't have to force it. The ebb and flow of stress and release allows change and growth to occur organically.

Make sure that the "on" and "off" times of your semesters coincide with when people naturally feel on and off. We'll get into the details of planning your calendar later, but just be aware that your semesters should mesh with the natural flow of life. If the schools in your community start back in September, then early October would be a perfect time to kick off your fall semester. That semester would last until mid-December, when things start winding down for Christmas. Be aware of how the people in your church think. Look at the structure of their lives and build on top of that. You will have much more success than if you try to force them into an inconvenient and unnatural mold. Because we have experienced it with our groups at The Journey and with the dozens of churches we've coached, we believe that small groups attenders grow best in short, concentrated bursts that work with their everyday lives. If you utilize that truth, you will lay the foundation for growth in your small groups system.

Big Idea #5: Think Promotion Months . . . Not Ongoing Sign-Ups

Convential Wisdom: *Small group sign-ups should be ongoing, so people can get involved with a group at any time.*

Reality: *A shorter, focused sign-up period increases small-group participation and excitement.*

So you've made a decision to implement the semester-based system in your church. You have three months on and one month off. Things are going great. People are plugged in and growing deeper in their relationship with God. New relationships are being formed. Everyone is fresh and energized. But what happens if someone new comes to your church in the middle of a semester? Can they get involved in a group? Logically, we would want to say, "Yes, of course! People can sign up and jump into a group at any point in time." But in reality, that doesn't work. Ongoing sign-ups will benefit neither that new person nor your overall small groups system. The power of Promotion Months overrides this conventional wisdom.

The Power of Promotion

Six weeks to a month before the time for your next group semester to begin, you will want to launch what we call the "promotion month." During this month, you will be able to focus like a laser on getting all of your attenders connected in groups, and thereby harness the amazing power of positive peer pressure. You can capitalize on the fact that everyone in your church will have his or her attention pointed in the same direction at the same time. During this month, you will want to preach on the importance of small groups, send church-wide emails about small groups and prepare dramas about small groups. Use every device at your disposal and take full advantage of the concentrated opportunity to focus your church's attention and energy on signing up for small groups.

Promotion Months . . .

Increase small-group participation
Raise small-group excitement
Decrease leader and member burnout
Utilize the natural flow of the calendar
Allow for concentrated, creative promotion

If you had ongoing sign-ups for your small groups, you would never be able to utilize the power of the promotion month. Just think about it; you might have half of the church already in small groups and half thinking about joining. Because of the divide, you wouldn't have even close to the same ability to focus your church's attention on connecting with a group as you do with promotion months. If you tried to have ongoing sign-ups, you would simply frustrate the half who is already in groups. And the positive peer pressure that comes with everyone getting involved at the same time would lose its spark for those who aren't yet in groups. A promotion month creates a unified sense of excitement and urgency that leads to sign-ups.

"So, What About the Guy . . . ?"

"So, what about the man, the woman, or the family that comes to my church after small groups have kicked off? They've missed the promotion month. Can they not get into a group?"

This is the most common question we get. It makes sense that you would want that new person to be able to get involved in a group right away. But here again, think about what your new people are used to, from their normal experiences within society. Say that the family in question has just moved to your town. They have a daughter who is a sophomore in college. When they get here, in the middle of March, they know that their daughter can't just jump right in at the local university. She will have to wait until the next semester. That's just the way things work. The family isn't upset by this reality because they understand how the system is structured.

On the same note, if someone comes to a church and they want to know when the next small groups begin, you will always be able to tell them that new groups get started in a month and a half. No matter when they come to your church, they should never have to wait more than a month and a half to sign up for a group. Here's how that works: Some of your small groups—the ones that aren't full—will stay open for two or three weeks after the semester kicks off. So by the time groups actually close to late joiners, there is only about a month and a half until sign-ups begin for the following semester. Of course the groups won't actually begin meeting for another month after that, but it really doesn't matter. Your new people who are eager to join a group will begin to feel connected as soon as they sign up, and they will enjoy being part of the promotion month that precedes the new semester.

We have never had a problem with someone being upset that they couldn't get into a group right away. Most of them are so excited that they will have the opportunity to start fresh with a brand-new group, rather than joining a group where everyone already knows everything about each other, that they are more than willing to wait. The key here is remembering to think from the outside in. The truth is that the average unchurched person who comes though your door doesn't think, *I need to get into a small group.* They only know what you tell them. If they come in or come to faith during the time when groups are already in full swing, you should say, "Good news! In a month and a half, you will be able to sign up for a growth group. Between now and then, keep plugging in here at the weekend service, read your Bible and share your faith." They will not think twice about waiting a month and a half to sign up for a group. In fact, they'll probably find comfort in it. Then, when it is time to sign up, the excitement around the promotion month will infuse them with an even greater desire to get connected.

Having eager new people come in during the semester is great. When your next promotion month rolls around, they will be the first to sign up. Their anticipation will help with the buzz of promotion month because they will cause your first week sign-up numbers to soar. If they are not so eager, positive peer pressure will give them the nudge they need to get involved. And all of your attenders who are just coming off of the semester will be ready to sign up again, especially the ones who are in groups that they didn't want to see end. The promotion month will give everyone time to rest and restore; and when it is time to kick off the new semester, they'll be raring to go.

By having a promotion month instead of ongoing sign-ups, you are going to greatly increase the success and effectiveness of your small groups system. Be willing to step away from conventional wisdom here. The benefit of plugging in the one guy who is adamant about starting in a group "right now" (which probably signals an underlying problem) is far outweighed by the overall benefit of getting everyone connected in a fresh way with each promotion month.

Through understanding and utilizing this truth, you are going to increase your small-group participation. You will raise excitement and passion in your church. You will decrease burnout among your small-group leaders. You will be working with people's natural state of ebb and flow by timing your semesters with the academic calendar. And you will be giving yourself the freedom to creatively focus on the value of small groups through your messages.

Promotion months will accelerate the spinning of your small groups system, so make sure you take this Big Idea to heart. When it comes to filling your groups, think promotion months . . . not ongoing sign-ups!

Big Idea #6: Think Church *of* Small Groups . . . Not *with* Small Groups

Conventional Wisdom: *Small groups are just one of many programs that the church offers to its attenders.*

Reality: *Small groups are exponentially more effective when they stand alone, rather than having to compete with other church programs.*

Have you ever noticed how easy it is for us to be our own worst enemy? Too often, we sabotage ourselves without even realizing it. We think we are moving through life—or through ministry—doing all we can to prosper and grow. But, if we were to look closely, most of us would find that we are unconsciously creating quite a bit of "drag" for ourselves. We have bad habits that keep us from being as productive as we could be, wrong thinking that has pointed us just off center of our desired target, and a tendency toward incessant busyness that has robbed us of our full potential in key areas of focus. This drag on our system is almost imperceptible to us. But when an onlooker points it out, we begin to realize what we could be accomplishing if it weren't there. Only in the reflection of our potential do we recognize the truth of our current reality.

What would the church look like if we all got serious about our focus? Imagine if each one of us made a commitment to concentrate only on those things that strengthen the Body of Christ individually and as a whole, refusing to get bogged down with distractions that quell our effectiveness. What if we eliminated all the drag? What kind of church would that be?

Two Types of Churches

When it comes to small groups, there are two primary types of churches—churches *with* small groups and churches *of* small groups.[1] Drag will subtly latch itself onto many churches when leaders make the conventional decision to operate *with* small groups. Let's take a closer look at the difference.

1. Church *with* Small Groups

A church *with* small groups offers its attenders a buffet of ministry options to choose from—different programs and ministries to meet various needs and occupy people's time. Small groups are just one of the many options. In addition to groups, the church *with* small groups may have a mid-week worship service, men's ministry events, women's ministry events, recovery programs, and ongoing adult education seminars. The list could go on and on.

2. Church *of* Small Groups

A church *of* small groups focuses on and runs all ministry through the small groups system. The church's attention is completely centered on the weekend service and small groups. Everything that happens in the church happens by way of these two entities. No other programs or extra ministries vie for attention in a way that could take away from or limit the effectiveness of the small groups.

Choose to Be a Church *of* Small Groups

If you want to see more than 30 percent to 40 percent of your attenders involved in a group, you need to make the decision to be a church of small groups. Otherwise, you will be acting as your own worst enemy and putting drag on your own system. When you decide to structure your system for growth, focus is the key. There is no way you can ask attender Joe Average to be at the weekend service, be at the mid-week service, go to the men's prayer breakfast on Friday morning and be in a small group. It's unrealistic. He only has so much time. When you create a culture that gives your attenders multiple options for how they want to engage in ministry, you do them a disservice. Here are a couple of scenarios we've seen happen time and time again.

Scenario One

Joe Average decides that he really wants to be part of a small group (since you've done such a good job convincing him of the benefits), but he doesn't want to miss the Wednesday night service, so he decides he'll do both. Maybe he'll even still try to make it to the Men's Prayer Breakfast. He's a go-getter. (By the way, only your most dedicated members will even try to fit in more than one activity outside of the Sunday service.) Suddenly, Joe has church on Sunday morning, small group on Monday night, mid-week service on Wednesday night, and the Men's Prayer Breakfast every other Friday. Not to mention a wife, three boys, a 60-hour a week job and membership in a bowling league. In no time at all, Joe will be burned out and discouraged. And you pushed him to it by asking him to take on a group in addition to the other ministries the church offers.

This scenario becomes even more frustrating as you begin to realize that small groups are a much better way to engage Joe in spiritual growth and help him form relationships than the mid-week service or the Men's Prayer Breakfast. You are cluttering his allegiance to a stronger ministry for the sake of weaker ones. Don't misunderstand. We are not saying that a mid-week service and men's ministry events are bad; they just aren't the best. They aren't as effective as small groups at engaging and growing your attenders. Not to mention, they skew your focus and put drag on a system that is trying to establish full participation in small groups. When you keep options in place, you are crowding out what can be great in the name of what is good. You can continue to accomplish the goals of these other ministries through a well-developed small groups system. But if you insist on having a church *with* small groups, you will have a church full of frustrated and discouraged Joes and Janes, only 30 percent to 40 percent of whom join your groups.

Scenario Two

Joe Average understands what you are saying about the importance of small groups, but meeting face to face with a group of new people is a little intimidating. And he's comfortable in the mid-week service. He even makes it to the Friday morning breakfast most of the time. Joe weighs his options and decides there's no way he could add anything else to his plate. He's stretched too thin already. Even though groups sound interesting, he likes the other programs he's involved in better.

When people have to choose small groups over other ministries and programs offered by the church, many will take the path of least resistance and say no to groups. By putting too many options on the table, you are shooting your system in the foot. There won't be any excitement around promotional months and group sign-ups, because only a fraction of your people will have the time or energy to be involved. No one will have the feeling that they'll be missing out on something special if they aren't in a group because so many other people aren't in a group either. After all, Joe isn't in a group. So Jane thinks she doesn't have to be. She's a new attender and doing well just to make it to church on Sunday mornings. And if she's going to be involved with anything else . . . well, she's always been interested in joining up with some kind of Celebrate Recovery program.

See how it works? It keeps going, too. Jane is new to your church. The recovery program (if she decides to get involved) is probably not going to close the back door for her. But if you could get her into a group, she would consistently be in an environment where she could form relationships with people, take on some responsibility and begin to grow deeper in her walk with God. She would be much more likely to become a regular attender, and then a member. But since you didn't create a small-group culture that would all but ensure her involvement, you left the back door wide open for her. Other programs of ministry simply aren't as effective and they will keep people from joining your groups.

In addition, the more ministries your church has competing with small groups, the more energy they take from you and your staff. Instead of being focused on groups, your time, effort and resources are spread too thin by trying to keep multiple ministries above water. But by focusing on groups and using groups as the primary platform for other ministries, you and your staff are able to be exponentially more efficient and effective with the limited time, energy and resources that you have.

I (Nelson) was working with Rick Warren at Saddleback Church in California when he made the tough decision to stop holding a Wednesday night service. At that time, Saddleback had about 14,000 regular attenders every weekend, and about 1,000 of them were involved in the mid-week service. Those 1,000 people loved the mid-week service. They were dedicated to it. They were used to it, because it had been a tradition in the churches where they grew up. However, Saddleback was in the process of creating a powerful small groups system and could see that this mid-week service was creating drag. Understandably, those 1,000 people attending mid-week could not commit to both. So, making the decision to be a church *of* small groups, Rick ended the mid-week service. Two years later, Saddleback had 20,000 people in small groups. Not a bad exchange.

You may have your heartstrings tied to some of the programs at your church. Step back and look at the larger perspective for a minute. Would you rather have 50 women coming to that monthly women's event or have those 50 women involved in and flourishing through consistent, vibrant, healthy small groups? Would you rather have 150 people sitting in the teaching environment of a Wednesday night service or have those 150 people engaged with other believers, growing and serving in a small group? They won't do both. This is another paradigm shift. If you believe that small groups are the best vehicle for growth and maturity, you have to make sure your people get in that vehicle. When you offer them the keys to 6 other vehicles at the same time, you undermine your system. They will only drive one. Which one do you want them in?

Activate Principle

If you give people too many options, their involvement will be so spread out that you won't have their full participation or momentum in any one area.

There's also a psychological element that comes in play. To begin creating a strong small groups culture in your church, you have to create excitement. Buzz is important. You have to let your people know how strongly you believe in the power of groups and how important it is for them to be involved. People in groups will start talking to those who aren't in groups about joining a group. New people will sense that they are going to miss out on something if they don't connect with a group. The overall impression is that groups are the way to go, so get on board! But if groups are just one of the options they have for ministry outside the weekend service, the energy surrounding groups will never be electric. Your people will have the impression that groups are simply there for those interested, not a vital part of the church's structure.

Are you beginning to see how, by being hesitant to let go of some old ways of thinking, you can doom your small groups system before it starts? How much sense does it make to create drag on your own system? To compete with yourself? Focus is the key to success. Everything you've been accomplishing in the other ministries that you are passionate about can run through the weekend service or small groups. At The Journey, we've made the decision that everything we do has to fit one of two criteria: It either has to expand the weekend service or advance small groups. If a ministry idea, program or suggestion doesn't directly do one of those two things, we don't allow it to distract us or slow us down by pulling sideways energy from the system. If you run groups as a lean machine, you are going to be more effective at reaching and keeping people, which will result in more growth and more life-change.

The Church as a Rocket Ship

If you think of your church as a pyramid of sorts, try flipping that pyramid on its side so that it resembles a rocket moving through the atmosphere. Think of the two halves of that rocket as the weekend service and small groups, and visualize anything else that tries to attach itself to the rocket as a force creating drag.

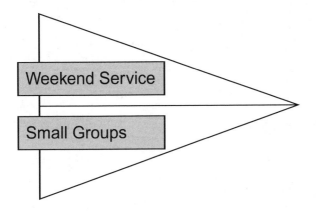

When you focus your energy on your two most effective avenues helping people move toward a fully developing relationship with Jesus—your weekend service and small groups—you will be able to create an atmosphere that God will pour His blessing on—an atmosphere you can move through without resistance. You can be perfect in implementing and running the small groups system we are going to outline, but if you allow your system to have the drag of additional competing systems, you will never see full participation.

How much value do you place on small groups? The answer to that question will determine whether you want to be a church *with* small groups or a church *of* small groups. If you have decided that you want to create a strong, healthy, fully participating group culture, ask yourself: *Is there anything I am doing in my church that is going to prevent us from getting 100 percent group participation?* If your focus is spread too wide, it's time to narrow it down to the two halves of that rocket. Stop expending sideways energy. Great people and great organizations do a few things extremely well.

Are you ready to produce some spiritual giants? Decide to be a church *of* small groups.

Note
1. Bill Donahue and Russ Robinson, *Building a Church of Small Groups: A Place Where Nobody Stands Alone* (Grand Rapids, MI: Zondervan. 2001).

Rethinking Small-Group Strategy

Big Idea #7: Think Easy . . . Not Hard

Conventional Wisdom: *People are willing to go through a multiple-step process to join a small group.*

Reality: *One-step sign-ups, which make getting into a group faster, easier and less intimidating, will greatly increase the number of people who decide to join a group.*

We live in an "easy" culture. Compared to past generations, we have it made. We have information at our fingertips anytime of the day or night. We can talk to anyone in any part of the world with the press of a button. We have machines that wash our clothes, our dishes and our cars. We have 24-hour superstores where we can get whatever we need the moment we need it. We are used to easy. Easy makes us happy.

Easy also makes the people who attend our churches happy. The more difficulty and stress you can keep from their lives, the better. Everyone who sets foot in your church is accustomed to streamlined processes. When they walk into a fast-food restaurant, they can order a "Combo 1" and know exactly what they are going to get. When they shop on Amazon.com, they can go through checkout with one click of the mouse. How is this possible? Because someone did the difficult back-end work required to set up a simple system for their benefit. So how about when they show up at your weekend service and decide they want to sign up for a small group? Is that easy for them too?

As a society, for better or for worse, we have become accustomed to taking the path of least resistance whenever it is available. If we do hit resistance, our desire and will have to kick in as we subconsciously evaluate how badly we want the end goal. If that resistance trumps our desire, we back down. It's a simple fact of current human nature. As you set up your small groups system, you can either choose to work with this fact and increase your sign-ups, or work against it and lose people in the cracks of resistance and difficulty.

One of the keys to creating a strong full-participation small groups system is to make groups easy to get into and easy to get out of. You make them easy to get into by establishing a one-step sign-up process, and easy to get out of by setting solid end times and end dates. Here, we'll focus on helping people into groups with simple sign-ups.

The Simple Sign-Up

When someone decides to sign up for a small group at your church, it should be an immediate, one-step process. Never, ever ask people to do multiple things to become part of a group. In our experience at The Journey, and in working with thousands of churches across the country, we have found that for every incremental step you add to the sign-up process, you exponentially decrease the number of people who will sign up.

Imagine a church that has 100 people in attendance on a given Sunday. That church is planning to start small groups soon, so the pastor preaches on relationships, builds excitement about groups and explains how important it is for everyone to get involved. The congregation gets fired up. They are abuzz with excitement. But what if the pastor then tells them that they can't sign up right away? Instead, they need to come to a group connection night during the week where they will learn how to actually get involved. Of those 100 people in attendance, approximately 50 percent will turn their current excitement into future action. So, about 50 people will show up—which means the pastor lost 50.

When connection night arrives, the pastor has to get those who came excited all over again and explain once again the significance of being in a group. Then he or she might give them a handout that outlines how to get involved or, even worse, give them a list of leaders' phone numbers and tell them to call a leader to sign up. This pastor, who had a 100-person congregation excited about small groups on Sunday morning, has hindered his or her own groups system by complicating the sign-up process. At best, the pastor will only get 25 percent to 30 percent of his or her people to commit to a group.

What if, on that Sunday morning, after getting the congregation revved up about groups, the pastor had given them the opportunity to sign up right then and there, in one easy step? Revved them up and then signed them up? No extra meetings to attend and no intimidating phone calls to make. The pastor would have had approximately 75 percent of the people in attendance join a group immediately! That's quite a difference. People like easy. And they like being able to take action while something is on their mind. By minimizing the number of steps potential joiners would have to take, this pastor could have set up his or her small groups for success. Instead, the pastor set himself or herself up for a continual struggle.

Activate Principle

With every step you add to the sign-up process,
you are going to lose a percentage of participation.

Creating a simple process for your attenders means that you are going to have to put some work into it. Part of the reason so many churches have difficult sign-up processes in place is because the pastor wants the people to do the work so that he or she doesn't have to. The staff wants the person who is interested in joining a group to call a leader for information so that they don't have to deal with it.

In a one-step sign-up system, your administrators and volunteers will have to put in some time making sure the right people get in the right groups and ensuring that group leaders are following up with those who join. But that's what we are called to do! As church leaders, we handle the administration so that our people can do the ministry and then benefit from the ministry.

This system was not created to make things easy on you. It was created to make things easy on the unbeliever who walks into your church one Sunday and has an urge to join a group; and easy on that sporadic attender who would like to be in a group but doesn't have time for a connection event; and easy on the shy, single guy who wants to be part of something but wouldn't dare call a leader he doesn't know unless bribed. People will use any excuse not to grow. We have to stop giving them those excuses.

What Does the One-Step Sign-Up Look Like?

So how do you create and implement a one-step sign-up process? What does it look like? You need two primary tools: a catalog and a connection card.

Small Groups Catalog

Create a catalog in which you list all of your upcoming small groups. The catalog doesn't have to be glossy and clever. It simply needs to be clear. There is no correlation between how artistic your catalog looks and what percentage of your people sign up. No one goes to a restaurant because the actual menu looks pretty, right? Choose being clear over being cute. List each group, the general location where it meets, the day and time it meets and who the leaders are. Give each group a number for sign-up purposes. For example, you might give Monday night groups identifying numbers like M01, M02, M03; Tuesday night groups T01, T02, T03. You can decide. Just make sure that all of your groups are listed and numbered. Keep it simple. You need to be able to change the catalog as things shift during the sign-up period.

Connection Card

Many of you may already use a Connection Card as your point of contact with your congregation. If you don't, we strongly encourage you to start. In *Fusion: Turning First-Time Guests into Fully Developing Church Members*, I (Nelson) detail the process for integrating a Connection Card into your culture.

In short, the Connection Card gives you the ability to get visitor information each week, gives your regular attenders a point of contact with you to report information changes, encourages people to take the next steps in their spiritual growth and gives you a place for small groups and volunteer sign-ups—all on one little (whatever size you want to make it) card. The Connection Card is a phenomenal tool, especially during small groups sign-ups, when you allow people to sign up for the group of their choice during the Sunday service in a space provided on the back of their card.

Let's go back to the pastor of that 100-person congregation. Imagine if he or she had the one-step sign-up in place. Here's what that Sunday would look like. After preaching on small groups and getting those 100 people fired up and ready to join, the pastor would tell them to look over the catalog (inside their bulletin) and find the group that interests them and fits their schedule. Then, to sign up, the pastor would tell them to write the number for that group in the space provided on the back of their Connection Card, which they will turn in when the offering is received. So, if Joe Average in the third row wanted to be in a men's group on Friday mornings, he would look at the catalog, find that group and write the identifying number (e.g., F01) in the space provided on his Connection Card. That's all he has to do. In a few days, the leader of that group will get in touch with him to thank him for signing up and to give him all of the important group details. With a one-step sign-up process, this pastor has multiplied his or her sign-up rate for groups before the congregation even walks out the door on Sunday morning.

One-Step, Multiple-Entry Points

While the sign-up process itself is one simple step, you will want to give your people a few options for how, where and when they take that step. We will discuss this in more detail in Part Two, but here's a quick overview for now. We have found that the three most effective points of entry are the Connection Card at the Sunday service, our website, and the small groups table at the Sunday service where people can meet group leaders, ask questions and get signed up.

1. Sunday Service

As we've detailed, the Sunday service is a great place to encourage people to choose their group and write down the number. While many of your attenders will sign up in the service, some will want to take the catalog home with them and look the groups over more closely. So you need to make sure you have other ways in place for them to easily take that one step when they are ready.

2. Website

At The Journey, we get a large number of our sign-ups through our website. On the website, they can look over descriptions and details for all of the groups and simply click on the one they are interested in to get signed up. A form will pop up asking them for their name and best contact information so that the leader of that group can get in touch with them. It's another option, but it's still one simple step.

3. Small Groups Table

Of course, every person is different. You will have a few people who really want to speak with a staff person or group leader before getting involved in a group. You need to provide them with that opportunity on site at your weekend service, not at a separate event. At The Journey, we have a small groups table at the back of the auditorium for the last several weeks leading up to the start of small groups, and then for a week or two after the groups actually begin. Each Sunday, a few of our group leaders stand at the table before and after each service to talk with anyone interested in discussing groups. Even at that table, we keep a one-step sign-up option in front of them—there are pens and index cards so that people can give us their name, contact information and the group number they want to join after they talk to the volunteers at the table.

The small groups table serves as the net to catch those people who may be slow to sign up or who may have questions. Those who need to meet a leader in this capacity before joining are usually in the last 25 percent of your sign-ups. This more targeted approach is not designed for your mainstream crowd but rather for the specific few who need a little extra encouragement.

With all of these entry points, the sign-up is still a one-step process. The person signing up doesn't have to attend anything extra or call anyone to get involved. They simply sign up, either at the service, online or at the small groups table, and then the ball is in your court to follow up. Still, while these options give your people choices, we recommend doing all you can to encourage them to sign up at the weekend service when the sentiment is fresh on their hearts.

Will They Come?

A common argument we hear in response to making small-group sign-up easy is, "If it's that easy to sign up, a lot of people will sign up and not show up." If you are doing your job correctly, that is simply not true. When your attenders sign up for a group, you start a process that, by default, keeps them locked into the decision they made. You will send them effective follow-up information. You'll be preaching on groups as the starting week for groups gets closer, to emphasize their importance. You will have past group members give testimonies from the stage. On the Sunday before groups start, you'll assure those who have signed up that they are going to have a great experience and you'll continue encouraging those who haven't signed up yet to get involved.

Positive peer pressure works wonders in getting those last few stragglers to jump in. Here's what we do: The last couple of Sundays before groups are set to kick off, we have everyone who has signed up for a group raise their hand. Not only does this make those who haven't signed up want to be part of the majority, but it is also a way of having those who have signed up make a public commitment that, yes, they are going to be part of a small group. They've made a commitment and they are excited about it.

Easy, one-step sign-ups allow you to connect with people you would never reach with more traditional sign-up structures. You open the gates for unbelievers, occasional attenders and even your regular attenders who will use any resistance as an excuse not to grow. Work with your people. When it comes to getting them into groups, think easy, not hard.

Big Idea #8: Think Ahead . . . Not Behind

Conventional Wisdom: *Thinking about upcoming small groups a month out gives you plenty of time to plan and prepare.*

Reality: *For groups to be successful, you need to start planning and preparing three to four months in advance of their start date.*

We've all been there. It happens all the time. You focus so much attention on your next big event, service or program that you are at a loss as to what happens when it's over. We like to call it "December 26 Syndrome." You know—the realization, tinged with surprise, that comes when the thing you've been consumed with ends and you wonder, *What do we do now?* For example, remember when churches across America implemented small groups focused on "40 Days of Purpose"? Everyone in those churches got in a small group. There was intention and excitement around making sure that people understood the principles of *The Purpose Driven Life*. But a year later, most of those same churches couldn't get anybody to join a group. Their focus had been so zeroed in on the "40 Days of Purpose" study that they didn't have a plan in place to keep their momentum going on Day 41.

There's magic in intentionally thinking two steps ahead. At The Journey, we are always reminding each other, "If you don't think ahead, you are going to fall behind."

Activate Principle
Average leaders focus on what happens next.
Extraordinary leaders focus on what happens after what happens next.

We know what you are thinking: *It takes all of my time and energy to do what needs to be done on a daily basis for the next service/promotion/event! How could I possibly think about and plan for what's going to happen after that?* The answer is simple. You need a system.

The Power of a SYSTEM

A good system saves you stress, time, energy and money. In fact, that's the acrostic you can use to help you remember exactly why systems are so important.

Save Yourself Stress Time Energy Money

All good systems give you the opportunity and ability to think ahead, to look at things through a wider lens. They provide you with checkpoints that allow you to continually plan for what happens after what happens next.

We've created a small groups system that allows you to always be preparing three to four months in advance for your next semester while you are successfully running your current semester. By learning how to Focus, Form, Fill and Facilitate, you will be able to effectively plan for the future without robbing any attention from the *now* (details in Part Two). The foundation of this system is built on having a Focus month at least three months before your small groups begin. During that month, you will do all of the necessary analysis, calendar work and game planning for the upcoming semester (see the "Focusing Your Groups" section). We're going to talk about putting a calendar in place that will keep your system rolling, keep you focused ahead and prevent you from falling behind. You will know every month, even every day, what you need to be doing to keep your small groups energized, consistent and successful, because you will have a system set up that will carry the load and save you stress, time, energy and money.

The Flywheel Principle

Just think about what small groups will look like in your church once you have a well-thought-out system in place—once you can plan in advance for them instead of always feeling like you are falling behind. Sure, getting the system going is going to take some work. You have to reap before you can sow. But once you have the system up and running, it does the work for you.

In his phenomenal book *Good to Great*, Jim Collins explains the power of the flywheel principle. A flywheel is a massive metal disk that is mounted horizontally on an axle. The disk usually weighs about 5,000 pounds. Getting a flywheel to start rotating on its axle is quite a challenge. As Jim Collins writes:

> Pushing with great effort, you get the flywheel to inch forward, moving almost imperceptibly at first . . . you keep pushing and, after two or three hours of persistent effort, you get the flywheel to complete one entire turn. . . . You keep pushing and the flywheel begins to move a bit faster, and with continued great effort, you move it around a second rotation. You keep pushing in a consistent direction. Three turns . . . four . . . five . . . six . . . the flywheel builds up speed . . . seven . . . eight . . . nine . . . ten . . . it builds momentum . . . eleven . . . twelve. . . . Then, at some point—breakthrough! The momentum of the thing kicks in your favor, hurling the flywheel forward . . . its own heavy weight working for you. . . . Each turn of the flywheel builds upon the work done earlier, compounding your investment and effort.[1]

Small groups are a lot like flywheels. Your first push—getting them off the ground your first semester while planning for the second semester—is going to take all of your energy. The second push will be a little easier. The third will be a little easier than the second. The point will come, as you get used to working with the flow of the Focus, Form, Fill and Facilitate system, when momentum will kick in and your small groups will spin in just the way you've set them up to. I (Nelson) rarely have to touch our small groups system anymore. At the beginning of each semester, I may ask four or five questions, or tweak a few minor things that aren't working quite right, but that's all. The system is in place and spinning, which has allowed us to trust others with running it. One hundred percent of our people are signing up. Lives are being touched and transformed. The flywheel is in motion.

This could never happen if we kept stress on ourselves by only working day to day or week to week, or even month to month. If just before a new semester we had to scramble for leader commitments, pull together a catalog and figure out how the weekend service might correlate with sign-up promotions all at the same time, we would expend a lot of extra time and energy and not get everything done. Not only that, but the resulting small groups semester would not be up to par for the participants. People recognize and appreciate the evidence of thorough back-end planning—the type of planning that is only possible when you have a system in place. When they see that creating a strong system has been worthy of your time, they know that it must be a system worthy of theirs!

Choose to be an extraordinary leader, not an average one. When it comes to setting up your small groups, always be thinking ahead so that you won't fall behind!

Big Idea #9: Think Full Staff Participation . . . Not Staff Specialist

Conventional Wisdom: *Have a small-group specialist on staff who runs the system so that no one else has to worry about it.*

Reality: *Every person on staff needs to have a part in small groups, especially the lead pastor.*

Most lead pastors share a common temptation when it comes to small groups: They want to turn the system over to someone else. They want to give it to a dedicated staff specialist so that they don't have to deal with it. We know! In theory, this doesn't sound like a bad idea. But the truth is that handing the system off too early is the worst thing a pastor can do for a small groups system. As a matter of fact, when it comes to implementing a successful small groups system, every single person on staff has to be involved, starting at the top.

Don't jump to any conclusions here. If you are the senior pastor of your church, you don't necessarily have to run the system, but you do have to own it. You have to be its number-one champion. You have to be engaged in how it is being implemented. And most important, you have to be *in* the system.

Does that mean you need to lead a group every single semester? No, not unless you want to. But you absolutely must be involved in a group and be quick to encourage everyone you come in contact with to do the same.

The Power of Pastor Buy-In

Recently, a church of 2,000-plus people contacted us, wondering if we could help them with their small groups system. They had tried everything but kicking and screaming to get their people in groups; but no matter what they did, they couldn't get more than 30 percent to sign up. Guess what the first question we asked was: "Is the pastor in a small group?" (He wasn't.)

Apparently, the lead pastor of this church had fallen into the kind of unhealthy thinking that many of us are susceptible to. He didn't want to be in a small group because he was hesitant to let members of his congregation get that close to him; he was afraid they would find something about him they didn't like. You know what? They probably would have! But that is all right. We are all human, and we're called not to be perfect but to let Jesus make us perfect in our weakness.

Ego issues are personal stumbling blocks that need to be brought before God. If a pastor chooses not to participate in a group in an attempt to keep an elusive distance, or for any other reason, the system will never work.

Activate Principle

Your church's attitude toward small groups will be a direct reflection of the senior pastor's attitude.

Not only must the pastor be ecstatic about and fully participating in small groups, but every member of the church staff must also do the same. Period. This is a team effort, not the show of a "small-group specialist." When the staff fully buys in to small groups, you have the ability and the credibility to emphasize groups in every area of your church. The worship leader can talk to team members about small groups while the community service person talks to participants about small groups while the Sunday coordinator talks to volunteers about small groups. Get the idea? Everyone is involved.

If members of the congregation can point to staff people who aren't part of a small group, then they automatically think it's not a priority in the church and they start coming up with reasons they can't be in one either. We have found that people will use any available excuse not to grow. So, at The Journey, we made a decision not to give them any.

We require all of our staff members to be in a small group. Most of them lead groups on their own initiative. In addition, most of our staff have small-group administrative responsibilities that require them to help form small groups each semester and give staff oversight and support to those groups as part of their position description (see "Forming Your Groups" section).

When your staff understands the importance and benefit of groups, they want to be a part of the system. Never forget: Small groups work from the top down. When the people running the church are excited about the system, the people in the church will get excited as well.

Take a minute to consider the alternative to full staff participation. Say you decide to start a small groups system or revamp the one you currently have, but you are so busy with other church obligations that there's no way you could run the system. So, early on, you hire a specialist to take charge. Everyone else on staff knows that the specialist is in control of groups, so they don't really think much about them. The mindset is not one of community and teamwork, but rather one of "let the guy getting a salary for groups deal with them." Inevitably, you or some people on staff decide they don't have time to even be in a group, and the deterioration begins. In this kind of small-group culture, you will never get more than 30 percent to 40 percent involvement.

Activate Principle

People will know what is important by what you do, not by what you say.

The fact is that people buy into the leader as a person before they buy into that leader's vision. If you, as a leader, aren't buying into your own vision for small groups, you can be sure that no one else will either, because they buy into you first. There's no shirking the responsibility. This all begins with you.

When Hiring a Staff Person Is Okay

Good news! There will come a point in the life of your small groups system when it is appropriate to hire a staff person. As the system grows and you start having somewhere between 300 to 500 people in groups, you will need someone to be in charge of all of the everyday details. Until this point, the senior pastor should "own" groups. Even if a dedicated volunteer is handling a lot of the work, groups are the pastor's responsibility until the first staff person is hired. Even then, as the baton is passed, the entire staff's level of excitement, involvement in and championing of groups has to remain consistent. Just because a staff person comes on board to run the ins and outs of the system doesn't mean that staff participation or excitement can wane. The pastor and every member of the staff should still spend 5 percent to 10 percent of their time and energy on groups. After all, by this point groups are the culture of your church. It's only natural that every staff member would continue to shoulder a little bit of his or her success.

Growing Organically

As your church becomes small groups centered, the system's growth will begin to happen organically. There are three things you can continually do to keep the soil fertile.

1. Encourage Staff Members to Keep Their "Groups Radar" Sharp

Every staff member should be making a habit of connecting people to groups and constantly encouraging new people they meet to sign up for a group. At every Sunday morning service, community project, fun event, children's ministry drop off, etc., the church staff should be connecting people with language such as, "Hey, Dave. How are you? So you've been at the church for three weeks now? Have you heard about our small groups? Let me introduce you to Ed. He's leading a great group . . . ." Church staff are always sparking interest in an attempt to spur uninvolved people into action.

2. Have Group Member Testimonies at the Weekend Service

Preface these testimonies with something like, "Ben and Sara are going to give a testimony now about how God has been working in their marriage. They are in Craig and Emily's small group . . ." Make small-group language something your people are used to hearing. The subtle implication being that if someone isn't involved in a small group, they are missing out on something big.

3. Hold Members Accountable for Small-Group Participation

At The Journey, small-group participation is a membership requirement. (For additional resources on developing a strong Membership Process, see this book's website at www.ChurchLeaderInsights.com/Activate.) As we saw with staff participation, you will never get new people (people from the crowd and congregation) involved in a system that your *members* haven't bought into. It's okay to ask your members to make groups a priority and then hold them to that commitment. Groups are an essential part of their spiritual growth. This doesn't mean they have to lead or be in a group every single semester. If some life circumstance is making commitment to a group difficult, they can take a semester off—which also goes for the church staff—but they are part of the system and love the culture. They are excited about groups, talk about groups and regularly attend or lead groups.

Remember, as a leader, your attitude and the staff's attitude about and involvement in the small groups system is the rudder that will direct the church's small groups journey. There is a definite trickle-down effect that comes into play. As you latch on to the vision, others will follow. So do your part. Take the lead. Think full staff participation, and you will be on the path to small-group success!

Note
   1. Jim Collins, *Good to Great* (New York: HarperCollins, 2001), pp. 164-165.

Rethinking Small-Group Leadership

Big Idea #10: Think Apprentice . . . Not Expert

Conventional Wisdom: *Group leaders need to be biblically knowledgeable, longtime Christians and must undergo extensive training in order to lead a group effectively.*

Reality: *Serving as an apprentice/coordinator in a group will prepare potential leaders to lead a life-changing small group on their own, regardless of how long they've been Christians or what their level of training and expertise.*

Church leaders tend to be control freaks. It's just the way we are built. Most of us have to work hard at learning to let go and delegate effectively. And we take great pains to make sure we only have the best, most qualified team of people around us. Of course, when it comes to church business and leadership, we *need* to be extremely careful about who we let into our inner circle. But if we ever want to create a successful small groups system, we have to let go of that tendency to control, especially when setting up the parameters for group leaders.

Are you ready for another paradigm shift? Your small-group leaders do not have to be longtime Christians in order to qualify to lead a group. They don't have to be gifted teachers or Bible whizzes either. You don't have to search out the best-dressed and most social people in your church and pursue them to be leaders. And you don't have to set up weeks of training to prepare leaders to take charge of their groups. When you put these kinds of high standards in place, you limit the pool of leaders you can draw from. Only a small fraction of your people would even qualify! Then, even some of these may want to run in the other direction because of the pressure and time demands your system imposes on them—and it is all unnecessary.

Think about the churches Paul planted. Within a matter of months, he would leave a young church in the hands of new leaders, most of whom had just become believers. He felt comfortable putting such leaders in charge because they had learned how to operate the church through watching and engaging with him. They were not the strongest candidates to lead a church. They had not been believers for very long. They had not undergone extensive training on how to handle every possible scenario they might be presented with . . . but Paul trusted them. Or, more pointedly, Paul trusted God with them.

So, how did Paul get these new leaders ready? What kind of requirements and standards did he put in place for them? Only one—that they watch what he was doing and do the same. In 1 Corinthians 11:1, Paul tells the young Corinthian leaders, "And you should follow my example, just as I follow Christ's." He called on these believers to serve as apprentices, knowing that when they had, they would be ready to be leaders.

Learn and Return

Jesus replied, "I assure you, the Son can do nothing by himself. He does only what he sees the Father doing. Whatever the Father does, the Son also does."

JOHN 5:19

The best way to raise leaders in your church is through "organic apprenticeship." You don't raise leaders through heavy training or through leadership development programs. You raise leaders by looking for the people who have been in your system and are familiar with it; those who are watching what you do and are eager to repeat it. We like to call this process of leadership development "organic apprenticeship" because there is a natural element to the way it happens. It's the way Jesus trained His disciples, and the way Paul trained his new church leaders. In John 13:15, Jesus said, "I have given you an example to follow. Do as I have done to you." In 1 Corinthians 4:16, Paul echoes Jesus' training philosophy: "So I ask you to follow my example and do as I do." So, what does that look like for your small groups?

As we will explore in further detail later, each of your groups should have a group coordinator. The coordinator is a person who assists the group leader during the semester in preparation for leading a group in the future. A coordinator helps the leader by emailing the group before each week's meeting, setting up a snack schedule and leading one or two group discussions during the semester. As a coordinator becomes immersed in the life of a group, learning from and helping a current leader, he or she is getting the training needed to lead a group the next semester. A coordinator learns by watching and by doing, not by sitting through hours of training or seminars.

This is why your small-group leaders need to know that they should always be looking for potential leaders within their group. Those potential leaders can become coordinators for their current group or for their group the next semester, and then they will be prepared to step up as group leaders after that. In essence, you are teaching your leaders to grow new leaders by learning to replace themselves in four steps:

1. I *do* and you *watch*.
2. I *do* and you *help*
3. You *do* and I *help*.
4. You *do* and I *applaud*.

You will pour into an initial set of leaders who will pour into other leaders who will in turn pour into other leaders, and on and on. Eventually, you will not even know all of the leaders in your church, but each one will have been raised through this organic process and have knowledge that is traceable to those first leaders you invested in and trusted as you learned to let go of the need to control.

Shaping Your Group Leaders

Again, we will go much deeper into the specifics of shaping your groups in Part Two, but keep these key principles in mind:

- Let your potential leaders know that your small groups are discussion-based, not lecture-based. In other words, they will not have to serve as a teacher, simply as a facilitator. By doing this, you will exponentially increase the number of people who are qualified to lead a group.

- Rely on good curriculum for theological foundation (see The Journey's "Approved Small-Group Curriculum" list at www.ActivateBook.com).

- Let your group leaders know that it is okay to say "I don't know" if faced with a question they can't answer. They should never try to make up an answer. Instead, they should seek out the answer from a pastor and report it back to the group the next week.

- Never ask your leaders to be experts . . . just facilitators.

Follow Christ's example in asking your leaders to follow your example. Develop leaders organically. Release the need to control every leader and every group as you discover the benefits of thinking *apprentice*, not expert!

Big Idea #11: Think Decentralization . . . Not Staff Control

Conventional Wisdom: *To ensure successful groups, paid staff must be in control.*

Reality: *Groups will multiply faster and be healthier when you trust God with your volunteer leaders and trust your volunteer leaders with your people.*

Maybe it's not our fault that we tend to be such control freaks. After all, we are just following conventional wisdom. From the outside looking in, it makes sense that you would want a staff person at least indirectly involved in every single group at your church, right? Otherwise, how are you going to make sure that all of the leaders are doing what they are supposed to be doing? How are you going to make sure that members are showing up and that life-change is happening? Conventional thinking says that you need to have a paid staff person in charge at every level to make sure everything is on track. There's only one problem with this way of thinking: It will completely debilitate your small groups system.

Activate Principle
As long as you have complete control over your system, you will only be able to go to a certain level before you plateau.

Learning to decentralize your small groups is essential to creating a system that can continue growing as your church grows. At The Journey, we learned this principle by working our way through a crisis of belief. When we first started our small groups system, we did everything we've already told you not to do when it comes to choosing leaders. Prospective group leaders had to fill out an application and they had to have an interview with a pastor. We didn't see the problem that was brewing, because things were going very well. We had 17 small groups and they were all full. Our church was growing.

But then we realized something terrifying: *Our church was growing.* When the time rolled around to start planning for the next semester of groups, we still had enough leaders for 17 strong, solid groups, but God was blessing our church in such a way that we needed to have at least 35 groups to accommodate all of the new people. So we freaked out. How were we going to put 35 groups in place when we only had 17 trained leaders? Thankfully, God opened our eyes to a truth that has become the backbone of our small groups system. We realized that we could call on potential leaders from within our current groups—people who may not look like the textbook icon of a group leader, but who really had a heart for small groups and a willingness to lead. We knew they weren't experts or Bible scholars. They hadn't filled out an application, had an interview or engaged in weeks of training. But we began to realize that was okay. If we would just be willing to let go and allow them to lead, we could have 35 groups instead of being limited to 17.

We would be lying if we said that relinquishing control over hand-picking the groups and leaders wasn't a little scary, but we knew we needed to try it. So, that semester, we had 35 groups. We were confident that 17 of them would be just fine, but the other 18 were something of an unknown commodity. All 35 groups filled up, and 34 of them were completely successful. We had to go in and do cleanup on one group. At the end of the semester, the question we had to answer for ourselves was: Would we rather have had 17 great groups that we had a higher level of control over, or 34 great groups and 1 that we had to do a little not-so-pleasant follow-up on? Obviously the answer was simple! Having 34 strong groups allowed more of our people to get connected, even if we didn't always have a hand in the weekly details of the group. From that moment on, it has been easy for us to let go. We saw what God could accomplish when we were willing to decentralize and trust our leaders with the people He was sending our way.

Activate Principle

You can structure for control or you can structure for growth,
but you cannot structure for both.

The Trust Issue

In Matthew 18:20, Jesus made us a promise. He said, "For where two or three are gathered together in My name, I am there in the midst of them" (*NKJV*). When you take that promise to heart, trusting your group leaders with your people becomes much easier. So what does this trust look like in action? Picture yourself letting go of some of the decisions regarding when and where your small groups meet and what they study. Instead of mandating such details from the top, you trust your leaders to establish the groups they want to establish, within a specific framework.

For example, say that you have a group leader who wants to lead a men's group that studies the book of James and plays basketball together on Tuesday mornings at 7:00 A.M. From your perspective, you may be able to come up with a list of reasons why that group won't work. But the reality is that if that group leader is interested in leading an early-morning James-studying basketball group, there might just be 15 other people in the church who would connect with that concept and jump on board. And that's a concept you would never have come up with if you forced all small-group possibilities to be filtered down through the hands of paid staff. We can pretend that we know the best all the time, or we can learn to trust the leadership—and the creative ideas—of our leaders.

Use Diversity to Encourage Growth

When you give your leaders the freedom to implement interesting, creative groups, you infuse your small groups system with life. There are numerous advantages to allowing your leaders to choose the theme and/or topic of their groups each semester. Here are a few:

- The availability of different topics decreases the chances that a group will become inwardly focused. People's interest in signing up for a specific topic will outweigh their desire to stay with one group leader indefinitely.

- Different types of groups (e.g., sports groups, moms' groups, writing groups) will make nonbelievers and seekers who are attending your church more willing to sign up. They may be more interested in meeting some new people and playing basketball than they are in studying James. At this point, that's fine. They may need to belong before they believe. The group's theme brings them in so that they can connect with believers and learn about God.

- People will grow faster when they are studying something they have an expressed interest in, allowing you to more easily identify future leaders and potential staff people.

- Men are more willing to join groups that are based on intriguing topics and built around creatively themed activities.

At The Journey, we allow our leaders to choose their own topics (which we approve) two out of the three semesters each year. During the fall semester the entire church studies the same topic. But even while we are all focused on the same thing, there are still different types of groups available. For example, we will have women's groups, artists' groups, professionals' groups, etc., all focusing on a concept that the church is studying as a whole, with tied-in teaching at the weekend service.

System Structure

Thanks to the power of a system, we have the ability to give our leaders huge amounts of freedom and still know that we will be pulled in if any problems arise. We will discuss the actual structure of our system in Part Two, but for all of you out there who are terrified by the thought of relinquishing hands-on control of your groups, rest assured that the system you will have in place is what allows you to let go with confidence. Through your network of group leaders, team leaders and staff, you are still completely plugged in; you just don't have to exercise growth-blocking control.

Though it may not always be *easy*, it is always *wise* to let go and let God. Trust Him with your leaders and trust your leaders with your people. Learn to decentralize, and watch your groups flourish!

Big Idea #12: Think Leader Multiplication . . . Not Group Multiplication

Conventional Wisdom: *The best way to increase the number of small groups in a church is to split existing groups.*

Reality: *Through the semester-based system and the practice of apprenticing, you can multiply groups naturally by multiplying leaders.*

What kind of images does the word "split" conjure up for you? Chopping up wood, maybe? Bad relationships? Bad hair? Nothing positive. "Split" is rarely used in conjunction with anything good. Yet many church leaders insist on "splitting" their groups in an effort to grow. Some, who have recognized the problem with this traditional terminology, say "multiply" instead. But the heart of their actions is the same. They aren't changing their practices, just the label. No matter what they call it, they are trying to grow groups by breaking them apart from the inside out.

The majority of churches doing small groups have fallen into the "splitting" trap, because it is grounded in conventional wisdom. They usually employ the idea in one of two ways: The first is to encourage group members to keep bringing new people in each and every week until the group is too large and has to split. The second is to let a group meet indefinitely until it starts to die of natural causes. Then half of the group goes one way and half goes another, each with the intention of growing new groups with the seeds of the old. Both of these approaches are unnecessarily messy, drawn out and inherently negative. There is a better way!

In Big Idea #4, we detailed the many reasons why a semester-based system is the most effective way to operate small groups. Not only does the system get more people involved by working with our already established calendars and life-flow, but it also grows groups naturally. If you learn to put the system we present in this book in place, you never have to split (or multiply) a group again. Instead of going in and breaking apart an existing, ongoing group in the name of growth, you let each semester run its course and identify new potential leaders for the next time around from those naturally ending groups. Then you will automatically have groups growing out of each other, because you are identifying new leaders in every group every semester.

A set start and end date for each semester allows you to multiply leaders on a regular schedule. And it makes your people comfortable joining, and changing, groups. They know that an end to the group is in sight when they sign up. As a matter of fact, that is probably what gives many of them the freedom to actually take the step.

Too often, as church leaders, we get so wrapped up in what we need to *do* to grow our people and our churches that we forget about the basics of human psychology—we forget about how God created us. We cannot work against the way people are wired. If we try to, we will always be fighting an uphill battle. Think about it from the perspective of your group members, especially those who are taking a leap of faith to get into a group in the first place. The mere idea of "splitting" the group when it becomes too large is scary for them. Maybe you feel like it shouldn't be, but it is. The way they see it, they don't have a say in the split or a solid date in front of them of when it is going to happen. Even though they may understand the positive benefits of a potential split, it still makes them uncomfortable. It breeds resistance.

On the other hand, if your people sign up for groups with a clear beginning and end date, they won't feel like the rug is being pulled out from under them when it is time for the group to stop. They are planning on it. They are excited that when the next semester rolls around, they can sign up for another group that interests them, fits their schedule or has a leader they'd like to study with. They'll see others they have been in past groups with stepping up to be leaders. Perhaps they're even thinking of doing the same the next semester. When you give people the parameters of a start and end date, you open a world of potential and possibility that is stagnated by long-term groups. The natural ebb and flow of each semester allows you to multiply groups without difficulty and negativity.

Raise Up, Don't Split Up

The nature of the system means that you should continually be on the lookout for new group leaders. The apprenticing process we've mentioned allows you to always have people in line (your current semester's group coordinators) to be leaders the next time around. You will also be asking your current leaders if they want to lead again and which people they would recommend as potential leaders from within their current group at the end of every semester. Let's look at an example.

Say you have 14 guys in a men's group during your fall semester. They know that the group has an end date—a date on the calendar when things will change. Toward the end of the semester, the group leader lets you know that one of the men in his group, Max, would make a strong leader. So you ask Max, "Would you be willing to lead a group next semester?" Max may say something like, "I'd like to take that step, but since it will be my first time, would it be okay if I asked Pete to lead with me?" You tell Max that Pete can be his co-leader/coordinator.

So, in the spring, Max and Pete lead a group together. Some of the men from last semester's group sign up with them. Some sign up with the leader from the previous semester. Some join completely different groups because of the meeting time or curriculum.

Look what has happened! Your groups have multiplied! And you haven't had to "split" anybody up. You didn't have to ask new people to join groups in the middle of a semester. You didn't have to wait until half of the group dropped off or moved away before you could grow them. The multiplication happened organically as you raised new leaders. And guess what? The next semester, after Pete has served as a co-leader or coordinator, he will be ready to lead a group on his own. And he'll be able to ask someone to be the co-leader/coordinator for his group. See how it works? As you lead others into leadership, the pipeline is always full.

Activate Principle
Multiply groups by identifying leaders.

Always keep the focus on identifying and raising up new group leaders. Then you will always have enough groups naturally. As you encourage people to lead, thereby asking them to take a step of spiritual growth, your small groups system will inherently be geared toward continual multiplication. With more leaders in place, you will have more room in more groups with every ensuing semester. God will bless and use this system—a system set up with a psychological understanding of how people tick and a biblical understanding of how to develop new leaders—to grow your church for His glory.

Keep the power of paradigms in mind. No one wants to split something they've become comfortable in. But everyone wants to raise up someone new. So allow your people to raise up and be raised up. Make it easier to happen by putting in place a start and end date for each semester. If you take this truth to heart, you will never again have to deal with the difficulty of multiplying by splitting. Remember, don't multiply groups: multiply leaders!

PART TWO

The Activate System

Introducing the Four *F*s:
Focus, Form, Fill and Facilitate

New ideas pass through three periods:
(1) It can't be done. (2) It probably can be done, but it's
not worth doing. (3) I knew it was a good idea all along!

ARTHUR C. CLARKE

Good ideas are common—what's uncommon are people
who'll work hard enough to bring them about.

ASHLEIGH BRILLIANT

Now you know our 12 Big Ideas. We hope that a few of them have caused you to have paradigm shifts—that they have caused you to look at the world of small groups in a new and unexpected way. You may not agree with every idea we've asked you to consider. That's okay, as long as they've caused you to examine the status quo. Or maybe you have already been thinking along the same lines yourself, but haven't known how to put your fresh ideas into practice in a practical way at your church. That's the thing about an idea: It is completely worthless until you put it into action. The hard work of innovation lies in taking the necessary steps to move a creative idea from the drawing board into real life.

Our goal for the rest of this book is to show you how we have applied these 12 Big Ideas in a practical way to the small groups system at The Journey, and teach you to do the same. We want to help you bring these ideas to life in your own system in a way that can transform your small groups ministry and, ultimately, your entire church. But let us give you fair warning: There will be work involved. While thinking about the 12 Big Ideas can be invigorating, actually applying them in a practical way demands some focused energy. You'll know it has been worth it when you begin to see the fruit of your labor in radically transformed lives. As the nineteenth-century clergyman Henry Ward Beecher said, "The ability to convert ideas to things is the secret of outward success." So, onward to conversion!

To get started, we need to take the 12 Big Ideas and break them up into four manageable, calendar-based steps: Focus, Form, Fill and Facilitate. As you will notice in the calendar outline below, the Four *F*s can be scheduled in separate months throughout the year. You will only be focusing on one *F* per month. This calendar flow keeps the system simple while making sure that you are on track month to month.

- **January: *Fill.*** January is your promotion month for the spring small groups semester, which will begin in mid-February and last until mid-April. (At The Journey, Fill/Promotion actually stretches from mid-January to mid-February.)

- **February: *Facilitate.*** Spring groups begin. Staff follows up to equip leaders and ensure that groups are going well (often lasts through mid-March).

- **March: *Focus.*** Begin planning for summer small groups.

- **April: *Form.*** Start forming your summer groups by asking people to be group leaders and/or hosts, and begin nailing down meeting locations, days, times and curriculums. (You can actually begin this step as early as late March.)

- **May: *Fill.*** Summer small groups promotion month. (Again, at The Journey, this promotion month actually runs mid-May to mid-June. You can tweak to fit your needs.)

- **June:** *Facilitate.* Summer groups begin. Staff follows up to equip leaders and ensure that groups are going well (often lasts through mid-July).

- **July:** *Focus.* Begin planning for fall small groups.

- **August:** *Form.* Start forming your fall groups by asking people to be group leaders and/or hosts, and begin nailing down meeting locations, days, times and curriculums. (You can actually begin this step as early as mid- to late-July.)

- **September:** *Fill.* Fall small groups promotion month.

- **October:** *Facilitate.* Fall groups begin. Staff follows up to equip leaders and ensure that groups are going well.

- **November:** *Focus.* Begin planning for spring small groups.

- **December:** *Form.* Start forming your spring small groups by asking people to be group leaders and/or hosts, and begin nailing down meeting locations, days, times and curriculums. (You can actually begin this step as early as mid-November.)

Take a few minutes now to really examine the steps. You'll notice that the Four *F*s repeat again and again throughout the year. You only have to have one *F* activated per month to keep your groups system healthy and growing. Take another look at the calendar through the lens of your three small-group semesters.

1. **Spring Semester:** February to April
2. **Summer Semester:** June to August
3. **Fall Semester:** October to December

Note that January, May and September are the three months of the year that groups don't meet. During these months, you will be filling groups for the upcoming semester, while giving current leaders and participants a break. As we discussed in Big Idea #4, the flow of the small groups calendar correlates with the calendar for the American educational system. The breaks coincide with semester breaks and holidays.

A little later, we will give you a more detailed calendar that will further illustrate just how this plays out. We'll show you how your Fall Semester groups end just prior to Christmas, thus giving participants a Christmas Break from late December until the end of January, and so forth. For now, start processing the calendar and begin ingraining the basic flow of the groups system we are presenting into your thinking.

Looking at a new concept from various angles always leads to better understanding. With that in mind, let's take a look at the Four *F*s from a bird's-eye view.

- **Step 1: *Focus.*** Determine the philosophy, strategy, goals and calendar for your upcoming small-group semester. This happens in March, July and November of each year.

- **Step 2: *Form.*** Recruit leaders, choose curricula and confirm the day, time and location of all groups. This happens mid-March to mid-April, mid-July to mid-August, and mid-November to mid-December.

- **Step 3: *Fill.*** Sign up people for groups through directed promotion. Give them the option to sign up at the Sunday service or online. Promotion months are mid-January to mid-February, mid-May to mid-June and September.

- **Step 4: *Facilitate.*** Begin and maintain groups while equipping and encouraging leaders. This happens in February, June and October.

As you'll see, our small groups system is detailed, but it is not complicated. We have worked very hard to be able to present you with a simple system that will save you stress, time, energy and money—as all good systems do. If you are in a church of fewer than 250, your groups system can be extremely simple while also being extremely powerful. If you are in a church of more than 250, your system may have to be more detailed, but you have the advantage of access to staff and volunteers who can help multiply the impact of what you are about to put in place.

With this overview of the Four Fs in mind, let's get down to the nuts and bolts of turning those 12 Big Ideas into big action. Here we go.

Focusing Your Groups

Focus

Don't begin until you count the cost. For who would begin construction of a building without first getting estimates and then checking to see if there is enough money to pay the bills? Otherwise, you might complete only the foundation before running out of funds. And then how everyone would laugh at you! They would say, "There's the person who started that building and ran out of money before it was finished!" Or what king would ever dream of going to war without first sitting down with his counselors and discussing whether his army of ten thousand is strong enough to defeat the twenty thousand soldiers who are marching against him? If he is not able, then while the enemy is still far away, he will send a delegation to discuss terms of peace.

LUKE 14:28-32

Often the difference between a successful person and a failure is not one has better abilities or ideas, but the courage that one has to bet on one's ideas, to take a calculated risk—and to act.

ANDRÉ MALRAUX

The biggest single mistake that we have seen enthusiastic, well-meaning church leaders make regarding small groups is to forge ahead without sufficient planning. Too many leaders reason, "We're just talking small groups. How difficult can it be, right?" Wrong! A successful semester-based system requires first and foremost that you think ahead. Practically speaking, you are always thinking one full semester in advance.

For instance, your fall semester might kick off the first week in October. By the first week in November, you have to already be planning for the spring semester even though there are still two months of group meetings left in the fall semester. Think ahead or you will fall behind. And yes, it is necessary to begin that early. You can't pull together leaders, curricula, meeting locations and times, and effectively mobilize the entire church to sign up, in just a few weeks. Planning a small groups semester that truly facilitates life-change takes months of prayer, thoughtful planning and hard work.

Plus, as your small groups system grows, the number of groups will grow, the number of people signed up for those groups will grow and your church will grow. Things get more complicated. You will get yourself into trouble if you don't intentionally schedule times to think strategically about your groups system—if you don't make sure your system is healthy and accomplishing what you want it to accomplish. In other words, you have to take the time to Focus.

Finding Focus

Three months out of every year are set aside as Focus months. At The Journey, we Focus in March, July and November—the months after our semesters begin. For example, since our summer semester begins in June, we start preparing for the fall semester in July, even though the fall semester isn't set to kick off until October. There are two simple reasons we choose the second month of a current semester to begin focusing on the upcoming semester.

First, *you can never start planning too early*. We would start earlier if we could, but it's important for our staff and our small groups team leaders to spend the first month of every semester focusing on the health of the newly started groups. Within the first month, you will be able to determine most of what you need to know about how successful a group is going to be. If groups are doing well and having good attendance, odds are that they will be effective and finish their 10- to 12-week lifespan with flying colors. Of course, team leaders will continue to check in weekly throughout the semester. But once you've passed the one-month mark of a new semester and things are on track, you can begin to Focus on the next semester.

Second, *you will find yourself in a time crunch if you don't start planning each semester at least three months in advance.* We have found that the key to pressure-free groups is allowing ourselves a month to plan and chart out the next semester; over a month to recruit and confirm leaders; and a month for promotion/sign-ups. That means three months of Focus. If you cut corners in this planning stage:

- You will have a difficult time confirming group leaders on short notice.
- You will end up asking the wrong people to lead, most likely out of desperation.
- You will make calendaring/scheduling mistakes.
- Your stress and anxiety levels will be very high.

So start planning early! One month after a semester begins, go into Focus mode for the next semester. Start by giving yourself and those staff members who are working with you on groups a couple of weeks to collect important information from previous semesters. Then, plan to come together in a Focus meeting. At The Journey, this is usually a two- to three-hour meeting when we lay everything on the table and brainstorm what we can do to make the next semester of groups better than the last. As we like to say, evaluation is the key to excellence. So, we start by evaluating current groups. Next, we start getting things in place for the upcoming semester: We set our calendar, define our goals and set the new semester's structure. Finally, we create a list of potential group leaders. By the time the Focus meeting is over, we have done the majority of our planning for the next semester. These "Five Aspects of Focus" are critical to your planning and preparation for each small groups semester. Let's take a closer look at each one.

Focus Step #1: Evaluate

True genius resides in the capacity for evaluation of uncertain, hazardous, and conflicting information.

WINSTON CHURCHILL

One hallmark of growing churches is that they are not afraid to ask, "How can we do it better?" In order for your next small groups semester to be the best it can be, you need to take a look back at the previous semester and ask, "How can we do it better?" That's the only way you will improve. It's how you can make sure that you are doing your part to be ready for the growth that God wants to give you.

Again, evaluation is the key to excellence. Start your evaluation by reviewing your last semester and asking yourself the following questions: What went right? What went wrong? How do we define and measure success? What records/information/statistics from last semester can we refer to for insight?

You can't evaluate what you don't measure. That's why it is extremely important to track your successes and failures in a variety of different areas.

Evaluate Sign-Ups

During our promotion months (Fill), we track and evaluate how many people sign up for a small group each week and how they sign up. That way, when it's time to Focus for the next semester, we have the actual sign-up data to refer to. In examining the data, we ask ourselves the following questions:

- Were there more sign-ups toward the beginning or the end of the promotion month?

- How many people signed up during the few open weeks after groups started meeting?

- Did sign-ups increase the week we had a small groups testimony or taught on the importance of godly relationships?

- How did most people sign up—on the back of their Connection Card, or online?

- If there is a significant decrease or increase in an area of sign-ups, did we do anything to set up or remove a barrier?

The insight you will gain through researching and analyzing these kinds of questions will be invaluable to you as you start planning your next semester.

In the early days of The Journey's small groups system, most of our people signed up at the Sunday service. They would look through the Growth Groups Catalog and note the groups they were interested in on the back of their Connection Card (our point of communication with each individual in the service). That's how almost two out of three people got connected with a group. But as the church grew, so did our number of groups. Suddenly, we saw a change. The percentage of people signing up at the Sunday service dropped while those signing up online soared. At first, we couldn't put our finger on it. Were we doing something wrong on Sunday? Were we doing something right online?

Eventually, we pinpointed what was happening. We had started offering a rather large number of groups (70 to 80 group options). That made it more difficult for people to review the catalog, consider their options and decide on a group during Sunday service. To have more time to make a decision, they had started taking their catalog home and signed up online later once they'd had the chance to look at all the choices. Now, the majority of our people sign up online, which is great! But if we hadn't been tracking this kind of information, we would have been behind the curve on what was going on in our own church when change started to occur.

Evaluate Group Success

Evaluating the success of your groups can be a lot of fun, but sometimes you do come face to face with groups that haven't worked so well. Never be afraid to ask yourself the hard questions. Take a truthful look as which groups were successful over the last semester and which ones were not. Is there a common thread among the groups that filled up the quickest? Is there a common thread among the groups that had low sign-ups or ultimately failed?

Usually, when you look for these common threads, you will find them. Make sure you examine all possible scenarios that could have led to success or failure, such as *location*. Allow us to state the obvious: The people in your church will find certain meeting locations more convenient than others. Currently, at The Journey, we have groups that meet in Manhattan, Brooklyn, Queens and Jersey City, as well as other metro New York locations. But we know that there are certain Manhattan locations that are by far the most convenient for the majority of our people, and therefore the most popular.

One of the mistakes we have made in the past is to have too many groups located in areas where few of our people live and/or work, and not enough in the areas most heavily populated by Journey attenders. For instance, one semester we ended up with too many groups in Queens and not enough in midtown Manhattan. As you might guess, several of the groups in Queens failed. Many of those groups failed while we quickly ran out of room in the midtown groups.

Activate Principle

Pinpoint the most convenient locations for your people and make sure the majority of your groups are concentrated there.

Day of the Week

Your culture will have certain days of the week that are more conducive to small groups. Journey attenders definitely prefer to attend groups on Tuesdays and Wednesdays. Mondays are next in line and Saturdays keep growing in popularity. Thursdays are not very popular, and we seldom if ever have more than one or two Friday groups. (Note that we don't have any Sunday groups so that we don't compete with the Sunday services, membership classes and baptisms.) Through many semesters of research, we understand what our people prefer and can plan groups accordingly, rather than try to force them into groups at inconvenient times.

As you begin to see what days your people prefer, make sure that the majority of your groups are scheduled for those days. The free market really kicks in to your advantage here. Most of your leaders will ask to lead on the day of the week that works best for them, and those requests will reflect the preferences of other like-minded people in the church. Having said that, make it a point to provide enough diversity. You do want everyone in your church to be able to find a group that works well for him or her.

During the week, evenings are best for most people. Accordingly, the majority of our groups begin around 7:00 P.M. However, other times of the day work better for different groups of people. We have found that stay-at-home moms really like morning or afternoon "Moms' Groups" where they can bring their young children. We have a number of professional groups at The Journey, and NYC professionals often have to work late nights. So, we've found it effective to have one or two breakfast groups each semester for those who can't get out of work early enough to attend an evening group.

Recently, due to a hectic schedule, I (Kerrick) decided to lead a lunchtime group. I honestly didn't think there would be much interest; so imagine my surprise when my group filled up almost immediately. Not only did 20 people sign up right away, but also the vast majority of them were artists representing the significant population of people in our church who work in the theater and artistic community. Now, I don't necessarily attract artists. I don't have an artistic bone in my body. But what I discovered was that we have a large number of aspiring actors, performers and dancers in our church who leave their days open for auditions. Most of them hold evening jobs, which keep them out of the majority of our small groups. A lunchtime group was perfect for them. My group was a big success. But if we tried to start 12 lunchtime groups, most of them would fail because evenings still work best for most people.

Study Topics

During two of the three yearly semesters (spring and summer), we give our small-group leaders freedom to choose what topic/ book/study they want to lead (with approval from our staff, of course). Most of the time our small-group leaders will choose topics that both appeal to others and are theologically sound. And just to be sure, we have an approved curricula list that we send to our leaders each semester. (For the latest copy of our approved curricula, visit www.ActivateBook.com.) We always make sure two studies in particular are being offered: *Experiencing God* by Henry Blackaby and *The Purpose Driven Life* by Rick Warren. We simply believe these to be solid studies that express foundational ideas of the Christian faith clearly and powerfully. If none of our leaders approach us first about leading these, we ask a few to take on one or the other. Groups doing these studies always fill up quickly.

We also like to make sure that we have at least one group each semester geared specifically for new believers and one that focuses on handling personal finances in a God-honoring way. In addition, premarital counseling is a big need in our church, so we always try to have at least one premarital counseling group during the spring and summer semesters. This group is a requirement for all couples that want a Journey pastor to marry them.

As you look at your church's culture, you will be able to determine what kinds of topics will best suit the needs and interests of your people. There will be times when topics that you thought would be great just don't get much fanfare. Let those topics go and concentrate on other theologically sound studies that attract people to your groups.

Allowing your leaders to choose curriculum is a bit of an art. While you obviously have to be careful about the kinds of studies used in your groups, you also have to hold your groups loosely enough to trust the judgment and interests of your leaders. Make sure you are walking the line between ensuring that your studies are theologically correct and capable of connecting with people in a meaningful way, and being dictatorial in telling people what topics to study.

You can keep everything to your standards by providing a list of approved curricula for your leaders to choose from and insisting that every topic idea not on the list will be approved by you and your staff. You want leaders to be able to lead groups on topics that interest them and you want people to join groups that are going to excite them. Your leaders will probably have a better idea of topics relevant to their peers and areas of particular spiritual interest/need than you do. Mandating curriculum rarely works.

Here's a great example: Recently, a potential small-group leader approached us with an idea for group study that really threw us. We thought it was horrible. We were sure that no one would sign up. Are you ready? He wanted to lead a group that would study a book he had found that compared the world views and philosophies of C. S. Lewis and Sigmund Freud.

Who would want to be in that group, right? Well, apparently quite a crowd. Twenty people signed up the first week. We had to close the group after just 6 days. It was our most popular group of the semester. Imagine that!

Ultimately, this group that we, "the pastors," knew would fail went really well and ended up producing several new members and leaders. People entered into interesting discussion about their faith and grew closer to God. Thank goodness we weren't so arrogant as to bring the hammer down on it at the beginning. This group serves as our reminder to let people try new and different things within the boundaries we have set. Sometimes you will be truly surprised by the interests, needs and desires of those in your church.

A quick note on topic promotion: When it comes to promoting your groups, it's not enough just to put the name of the book or study in the catalog and expect people to sign up. Find a person on your staff or in your church who is good at writing promotional copy and have him or her write some exciting and engaging descriptions for each group. Address questions such as, "Why should I be interested in this topic? What will being in this group do for me?" These descriptions, which will appear not only in the catalog but also on your website, should be no longer than two to three sentences each.

Types of Groups

We have found that having different types of groups for different types of people creates excitement and motivates more people to sign up. At The Journey, we do our best to offer a wide variety of groups each semester, such as:

- general groups (open to everyone)
- men's groups
- women's groups
- couples' groups
- artist groups
- professional groups
- community service groups
- college groups
- athletic groups
- moms' groups
- premarital counseling groups
- new believer groups
- groups that study specific books of the Bible
- groups that study approved Christian books
- groups that use video curriculum
- groups that build on the message from the previous Sunday's service

Obviously, you can't offer every type of group every semester, but the point is to offer a wide variety.

Each semester we aim to have close to 60 percent of our groups identified as General groups. General groups are not specialized in any way. Anyone can join. In the past, we have made the mistake of having too many of a specific type of group. For instance, if we were to designate 50 percent of our groups as artist groups, we probably wouldn't be able to fill them. We would also, by default, be limiting the number of groups available to non-artists. Make sure your group types correlate with your people types and with their interests, which again goes back to evaluating previous semesters.

The following chart lists a recent breakdown of group types at The Journey:

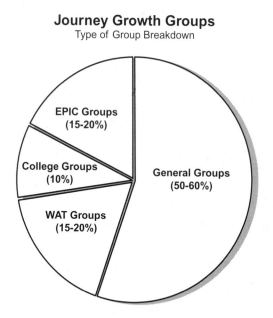

Journey Growth Groups
Type of Group Breakdown

EPIC Groups (15-20%)

College Groups (10%)

WAT Groups (15-20%)

General Groups (50-60%)

Number of Groups

It is possible that you might form more groups than you have people to fill them. That's okay; you were just dreaming big. If you see that your groups are not filling, check to see if this is a reason. If it is, there are steps you can take to solve the problem during the semester, such as combining groups (See Section Four, "Facilitate"). During this Focus stage, put some real thought into planning the appropriate number of groups. We will look at how to determine the right number for your church in more detail later.

Individual Leaders

Sometimes a group will fail, and it will be difficult to figure out why. Perhaps the location, day, time, topic and type were all good, but something went wrong. In these cases, you may be dealing with a leader problem. Was the leader lazy? Did he or she not do enough to promote his group and encourage people to sign up? Is the leader an odd character that people may not relate to? Does his or her personality push people away, instead of attracting them? If you can trace a group's failure back to a problem with the leader, you need to diplomatically keep that person from leading a group again. Or, at the very least, have a serious (but compassionate) conversation with the person about the problem before letting him or her lead again. Remember, one bad group experience can turn a person off to groups—even to your church—forever.

Leader Training

Don't forget to evaluate Leader Training. (Read more about Leader Training in Section Four, "Facilitate.") What did you do right during the latest training session? Did training lack in any area? Parts of the training for leaders may change each semester based on issues you ran into the previous semester. Listen to the needs of your current group leaders and involved staff as you plan the topics to focus on during your next training session.

When it comes to evaluating your groups effectively, avoid the trap of relying too heavily on your own discernment, and solely on statistics. The best source of information about your groups is feedback from the people who were involved during the semester in question. They are the ones who can truly let you know whether or not the groups successfully fulfilled their purpose.

At The Journey, we send an end-of-semester email to everyone who signed up for a group, asking them to fill out an online survey about their experience (see the following chart). We let people know up front that it will take only a minute or so to complete, and then we ask them 11 simple questions. This survey always gives us invaluable insight into what worked and what didn't. We get a true look into what parts of our small groups system are frustrating to group attenders and what they most appreciate. Such feedback is a great tool in our evaluation toolkit.

Fall Growth-Group Survey

Tell Us About Your Growth-Group Experience

Please take a few moments to complete this short survey about your Growth Group experience this semester at The Journey. Your answers will help us make Growth Groups better for everyone.

1. Name?

2. Which of the following best describes your involvement in your Growth Group?

3. How would you describe the spiritual growth you experienced through your Growth Group?

4. How would you best describe the people you met in your Growth Group?

5. How would you describe your overall Growth Group experience this Fall?

6. What is the most important factor that you consider when signing up for a group?

7. Are you planning on signing up for a Spring Growth Group? (Sign-ups for Spring Growth Groups begin in January.)

8. Would you be willing to lead or host a Growth Group in your apartment in the future?

9. What has been the best part of being in a Journey Growth Group?

10. As we prepare for Spring Growth Groups, what is one thing you would tell someone who is considering signing up for a Growth Group?

11. Is there anything else that you would like to tell us about your Growth Group experience?

Provided by www.surveymonkey.com

Focus Step #2: Set Your Calendar

Once you've evaluated your previous small groups semester and made appropriate adjustments, it's time to set your calendar for the upcoming semester. You and your team need to put all of the important dates for the upcoming semester in writing. And we do mean every single date!

Create a calendar that covers at least six months. If it is July, and you are starting to plan for your fall semester, create a calendar that runs from July through December. If you are planning for your spring semester, create a calendar that runs from November through April. If you are planning for your summer semester, create a calendar that runs from March through August. (Your calendar can cover a longer length of time, but don't chart less than a six-month cycle.)

We recommend setting aside some time once a year to do the detailed work of creating a yearlong small groups calendar. We like to do this each July. If you take the time to create a yearlong calendar, you won't have to start from scratch when it is time to set your calendar for the spring and summer semesters; you'll just have to review and edit the yearlong calendar you've already established. Regardless of whether you choose to create a yearlong calendar at this point, at least get all of the important groups dates set six months in advance.

1. Start by putting the biggest dates on the calendar. These will include:

   · When you will train small groups leaders
   · When your groups will begin and end
   · When you will have small groups sign-ups

2. Next, put down dates for all of the "less significant" items. Trust us, you need to get all of these on your calendar.

- Deadlines for asking/confirming small groups leaders
- Dates for staffed small groups table at Sunday service
- Date groups catalog and website need to be finalized
- Promotional email schedule (emails encouraging people to sign up)
- Small groups leaders email schedule, including topics (these are weekly emails sent to leaders throughout the semester)
- Dates for Sunday sermons on small groups or relationships
- Dates for other small groups focus during the Sunday services (dramas/videos/testimonies)
- Dates for the team leader meetings and staff small groups meetings

Carefully thinking through your calendar will pay off in a big way as you continue to develop your small groups system. For a complete sample calendar from The Journey, visit www.ActivateBook.com.

Focus Step #3: Set Your Goals

Without goals, and plans to reach them, you are like a ship that has set sail with no destination.

FITZHUGH DODSON

If you aim for nothing, you will hit nothing. As in so many areas of life and ministry, setting clear goals is an imperative part of the Focus process. You need to set high but achievable goals for your upcoming semester. You will set goals in several areas, and many of them will be interconnected. What you set out to achieve in one area will influence what you need to achieve in another. Plan to set goals for average

Sunday attendance; group sign-ups; the number of groups and group leaders, team leaders and coaches—all based on the small groups structure you have in place. Let's dive in and break this down.

Average Sunday Attendance Goal

What do you want your average Sunday attendance to be during the upcoming small groups semester? Does this seem like a strange place to start? It's not. Think about it. The primary aim of the groups system is not to bring new people into your church (although it can help in that area), but to get those who attend the Sunday service—even only sometimes—plugged in and connected. Groups complement the work of assimilation, not evangelism. Odds are that most of the people who sign up for your groups will already be attending at least one Sunday service during your promotion month. So your group sign-ups goal (which we will get to momentarily) will be dependent on knowing how many people attend your church over the course of your small groups promotion (Fill) month.

You have to secure a clear average attendance goal before you can set any of your group specific goals. Of course, this means that the lead or senior pastor needs to play an integral role in the Focus process. As a team, look at trends over the past few years and seek the Holy Spirit's guidance as you set Sunday attendance goals for the upcoming semester. Once you nail down that number, it will help you set your goals in other group-specific areas.

Sign-Ups Goal

Your sign-ups goal should surpass your average Sunday attendance goal. Did you catch that? You should expect more people to sign up for groups than attend your service on any average Sunday. Remember your Big Number. As we said earlier, the number of individuals who attend your church over the course of three months will be much larger than the number of people who attend your church on a given Sunday. You are trying to reach that larger pool. You want everyone who has come through your doors or called your church home in the last three months to sign up for a small group.

For example, let's say that you set a goal to average 150 people at your Sunday services during the upcoming semester. That means you will have perhaps 195 or more individual people who will attend your church over the course of a given month. So you would want to set a goal of having about 175 people sign up for groups, with the hope that your average Sunday attendance will grow as a result of more people getting more connected. (The only exception to this rule may come during the summer semester, when your percentage of sign-ups may be slightly smaller due to travel schedules and vacations.)

Activate Principle
Your sign-ups goal should surpass your average Sunday attendance goal.

Groups Goal

Once you've set your sign-ups goal, you are ready to determine how many groups you'd like to have available. Remember from Big Idea #2 that the ideal size for each small group is 12 to 15 people. Since some sign-ups will never show up, and not everyone who is committed will be able to attend every week, we suggest allowing as many as 16 to 20 people to sign up for most groups. Then there will be 12 to 15 people actually in attendance each week. To set this goal, you need to establish both the minimum number of groups you need to have to provide adequate space for your sign-ups goal and the maximum number of groups you can have. Here's how you do it:

• *Minimum Number of Groups:* Divide your sign-ups goal by 15.
• *Maximum Number of Groups:* Divide your sign-ups goal by 12.

Say that you set a goal to average 150 people at your Sunday services during the upcoming semester. Based on that goal, you set another goal to have 175 people sign up for groups. To figure out how many groups you should have, divide 175 by both 12 and 15. That gives you an accurate range. You need a minimum of 11 groups and a maximum of 15 groups in place for the upcoming semester. This formula works whether you are a church of 60 or 6,000.

Never, never, never make the mistake of not having enough groups in place for everyone in your church to get plugged in. That is the unpardonable sin when it comes to small groups. You can always combine groups if you realize that you're offering too many. But if you don't have room for everyone in your church to sign up for a small group, your rectifying options are much more limited.

Attendance Goal	Groups Needed
125	8 to 10
175	11 to 15
250	16 to 21
500	33 to 42
750	50 to 63
1000	66 to 83
2000	133 to 167
3000	200 to 250

Once you set the number for how many groups you want to have, you should set an equally aggressive goal for the number of leaders you want to have in your system. This requires an understanding of small groups structure.

Groups Structure

Creating a scalable growth structure as your church grows is key. So, before you can set your leadership goals, you need to set them within a structure that will allow plenty of room for growth as God blesses your church with more attenders, more groups and more group members. For churches with fewer than 20 groups, the structure can be very simple. Basically, the groups pastor is the structure. All groups report directly to him. However, as the groups system grows, a more intentional structure becomes necessary. Why?

Structure is necessary for accountability. Group leaders are not meant to be lone rangers within your system, doing whatever they feel like doing. At The Journey, we ask our small groups leaders to do four things: (1) pray for group members once a day, (2) lead the group once a week, (3) meet with their team leader in a Growth Group Huddle once a semester, and (4) work with their team leader and staff to form new groups from their current group toward the end of each semester.

A structure in which every leader is contacted at least once a month allows for accountability.

Good structure promotes communication. A structure in which a group leader has regular conversations with his or her "upline," or team leader, allows for questions to be answered quickly, last-minute issues to be addressed and life-changing stories to be shared. In a strong structure, every leader feels like he or she is being supported.

Good structure promotes expansion of the groups system. As group leaders get busy running the weekly operations of their group, they may forget important responsibilities like raising up new leaders or leading their group to do evangelism or serve in the church. A good structure has built-in commitment reminders for the leader.

Good structure minimizes problems. Regardless of the groups system you establish, there will be the occasional problem. However, every problem that is caught and dealt with early enough can be converted into an opportunity. Since every group leader is meeting with his or her upline support on a regular basis, problems can be caught and handled before they reach the crisis point.

So how can you structure your small groups for success? Well, since every church is unique, every structure is unique. There is no "one size fits all." You will want to make sure that at a minimum your structure can accomplish the four benefits we've just discussed. Next you'll see The Journey's structure. We suggest taking this and adapting it to your situation.

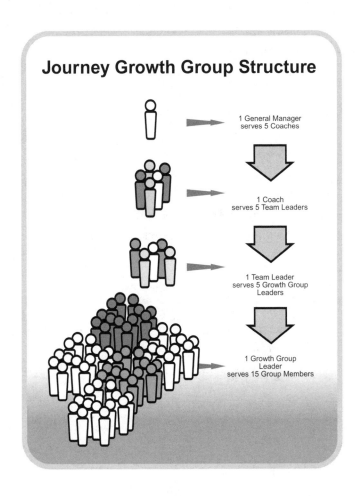

Journey Growth Group Structure

1 General Manager
serves 5 Coaches

1 Coach
serves 5 Team Leaders

1 Team Leader
serves 5 Growth Group
Leaders

1 Growth Group
Leader
serves 15 Group Members

Now, let's define each structural level. You will be setting goals for each.

Group Coordinator (Not Pictured)

The group coordinator is a group member who volunteers to assist the group leaders with basic administrative and organizational tasks throughout the semester. When possible, the coordinator should be someone interested in being a leader in the future. However, since this position is often not filled until early in the semester, there's no guarantee that a person who becomes coordinator will be interested in taking on more future leadership.

Commitment: One semester

Requirements:
1. Must be a regular church attender (although not necessarily a member).
2. Must be interested in and moving toward membership in the church.
3. Must be selected and approved by the group leader.
4. Must be willing to attend group leaders training.

Responsibilities:
1. Pray for group members every day.
2. Assist the group leader with organizational tasks every week (reminder emails, prayer request distribution, etc.).
3. Facilitate group discussion once or twice a semester.

Group Leader

Group leaders are the frontline leaders in your structure. They have direct impact on 15 to 20 group attenders every week. Group leaders require a high level of support.

Commitment: One semester

Requirements:
1. Must be a church member. (A first-time leader can be a regular attender headed toward membership.)
2. Must have been a member of a previous Journey Growth Group.
3. Must have served as a coordinator in the past.
4. Must be willing to attend group leaders training.
5. Must be committed to raising new leaders.

Responsibilities:
1. Pray for group members once a day.
2. Facilitate group discussion once a week.
3. Meet with team leader once a month.
4. Recommend at least one new leader from current group once a semester.

Team Leaders

Each team leader oversees five groups, or four groups plus their own group if currently leading. A team leader has been a group leader before and understands the groups system. For some churches, a team leader may be a part-time staff person; but for most churches, this is still a volunteer position.

Commitment: 2 to 3 semesters

Requirements:
1. Must be a fully engaged member.
2. Must be committed to tithing.
3. Must have led a Journey Growth Group.

4. Must be committed to the groups strategy.
5. Must have a willingness to meet monthly to manage the groups system.
6. Must be committed to raising new leaders.

Responsibilities:
1. Pray for group leaders each day.
2. Communicate with group leaders once a week by phone, email or in person.
3. Meet with group leaders once a month.
4. Form new groups once a semester.

Groups Coach

A coach oversees five to seven team leaders and gives overall support to the groups system. For most churches, this will be a full-time, paid staff position; but some churches may have strong volunteer coaches.

Commitment: Ongoing

Requirements:
1. Must fulfill all team leader requirements.
2. Must have served as a team leader.
3. Must have unshakable commitment to the groups system.

Responsibilities:
1. Pray for team leaders once a day.
2. Communicate with team leaders once a week.
3. Meet with team leaders once a month.
4. Form groups to meet the church's goals once a semester.

Notice that there is a timeline commitment for each position. When someone is invited to lead a group, he or she is being invited to lead for one semester only—not for the next year or for as long as the person attends the church. If a person does a good job leading, he or she can always be invited to lead again. If a person does a poor job leading, you can thank him or her and not invite that person to lead in the future. Building a timeline into your structure solves a lot of problems by keeping poor leaders from constant service and preventing burnout of good leaders. Even the best group leader should only lead two semesters in a row before taking a break.

When it comes to responsibilities for each position, keep the to-do list to a minimum. Ask each level to do no more than four things. The goal is to be clear and simple in what you require of your leaders and what kind of commitments they are making. We advise asking all of your leaders, in each of the capacities, to sign a covenant that details the commitments they are making. (For electronic copies of all position descriptions and covenants, visit www.ActivateBook.com.)

Whatever structure you choose, make sure that it can grow as your church grows. You may eventually need to form even higher levels of leadership. Although we are not there yet, we know that as God continues to bless The Journey and our small groups system, we will one day need to add a leadership level above the coach—the general manager. As you can see, in positive expectation, we have already listed this position on our charts. The general manager position will be a staff position overseeing up to five staff coaches. This person will need to come in when our small groups system hits 6,000 in groups. But until then, the structure defined above is exactly what's needed.

Now, with a working knowledge of the small groups structure in place, you are ready to begin setting goals for how many of these group leaders, team leaders and coaches you would like to have.

Small Groups Leaders Goal

Every small group needs at least one leader. But your goal for group leaders should far exceed the number of groups you are offering.

Why? You can never have too many small groups leaders; it's impossible. The more leaders you have, the more potential groups you have and the greater the likelihood of your church continuing to raise up new leaders.

Our goal at The Journey is to have one-and-a-half as many small-group leaders as we have groups. Of course, there are some groups that will have a solo leader. That always happens. But we like for at least half of our groups to be co-led or, at a minimum, have a leader and a coordinator. If a small-group leader doesn't have a coordinator when groups begin, we challenge him or her to find one from within the group as quickly as possible.

If our goal was to get 1,100 people to sign up for groups, then our small groups goal might be 80 groups. So, if I wanted to have at least half of those groups equipped with co-leaders and coordinators before the groups begin, I would need at least 120 people lined up to help lead groups. One time, we set a goal of 80 groups for a semester and were able to secure 136 small-group leaders before the semester began. We consider that a blessing! We have eager leaders in the pipeline.

Think strategically about how you put co-leaders in place. Sometimes you will have co-leaders that are a natural fit, like a husband and wife, or two best friends. Often you have someone who is leading a small group for the first time, or maybe a leader about whom you have a few lingering doubts. Pair those people with a co-leader who is stronger than they are. I've never met a small-group leader who didn't want a co-leader when we made the suggestion. Having someone else to help shoulder the responsibility of leading a group eases quite a bit of pressure. Everyone enjoys having someone serve with him or her and share the workload. (More on pairing up co-leaders in Section Two, "Form.")

Team Leader's Goal
Setting a goal for your number of team leaders (and coaches) will not be a matter of concern if you are just beginning your small groups struc-

ture or if you only have a few groups in place. If your goal is to have fewer than 175 people sign up for groups, you are not ready to expand your structure to include these positions just yet. But that doesn't mean you shouldn't already be looking for good candidates to fill those spots when you are ready.

If you have 15 groups at your church, you need at least 3 team leaders to help you manage those groups. Your 15 groups would be broken down into 3 teams led by different team leaders. As with co-leaders, it is also preferable to have team co-leaders who work together. You could have as many as 6 team leaders leading the 3 teams of groups. This is a great option when working with team leaders who are busy with many other obligations. So, if you were expecting 1,100 sign-ups with a goal of 80 groups, how many team leaders would you need? Just take the number of groups and divide it by 5 (the number of groups that each team leader can manage) and you get 16. You would need a minimum of 16 team leaders to help you manage 80 groups. Make sense?

But remember, just like with your small groups leaders, you can never have too many team leaders. At The Journey, we meet with our team leaders once a month and invest in them at the highest level (through accountability, training, resources, and so forth). We also hold our team leaders to extremely high standards (even higher than those of membership), surpassed only by our staff standards. If your goal is 80 groups, you should aim to have as many as 32 team leaders so that you can invest in them and they can, in return, invest in your small groups leaders.

Coach's Goal

The pastor or staff person in charge of the small groups system can act as a coach, effectively managing up to 5 or 6 team leader teams, or essentially close to 25 to 30 groups. On the same note, we do not hire staff people to serve solely as small-group coaches, but we do expect most of the staff people we hire to take on a small groups component as a part of their job description—often that is as a coach.

At The Journey, we like our staff coaches to lead a team of groups in their specific area of interest. For example, our worship arts pastor is the small groups coach for arts-related groups at The Journey. Another staff person is the coach for our community service-related small groups. A younger staff person might be the coach for college-age small groups. Then, we have multiple staff who serve as coaches for our general groups, which make up the majority of our groups.

If our goal is to have 1,100 people sign up for 80 groups, and we want to have at least 120 small groups leaders who are managed by more than 16 team leaders, we would need a minimum of 4 staff people dedicated to being small groups coaches (see the breakdown in the chart below). These coaches would work closely with and report to the small groups pastor or the staff person leading the small groups system.

Sample Small-Groups Goals Breakdown

Next is a blank scalable goals pyramid for you to reference. Write in your numbers for the upcoming semester. What are your goals?

Scalable Small-Group Structure

Goal setting is an act of faith. It's natural to feel a little outside of your comfort zone. Set goals that will stretch you and allow God to work in your church in a big way.

Focus Step #4: Set Your Structure

Setting your structure involves more than determining how your system is set up. Structure sprawls into the very details of defining exactly what your groups will look like in the upcoming semester. What types of groups will you offer? How many of each type? Where will your groups be located? What curricula will be used? What staff people will be involved, and in what capacities? All of these questions fall into your structure discussion. Using what you've learned from the past semesters, and with your goals clearly laid out in front of you, you are ready to set your structure.

As we mentioned earlier, every fall semester, all of our small groups at The Journey take part in what we call a church-wide campaign. Simply put, all of our groups study the same curriculum during the semester, and that curriculum is connected with the weekly teaching. In the past, we've done campaigns with topics/studies like "40 Days of Purpose"; the Sermon on the Mount; a series on what the Bible says about faith; a series on the power of influence; and even a series called "The Challenge of the New Testament," in which all of our groups read through the entire New Testament in 63 days and discussed their reading and the connected Sunday teaching in their small groups. (For a list of additional sermon series we've used as church-wide campaigns, visit www.Activate Book.com.) Because of the church-wide campaign, our fall groups are a little easier to structure. We provide an identical semester syllabus to all of our groups, and we don't have to worry about approving different curricula or making sure that certain subjects are covered.

Structuring our spring and summer semesters is a little more involved. During these two semesters, we allow our leaders to choose whatever approved curriculum the Holy Spirit lays on their hearts. We assume that if it's something they are interested in or passionate about, others will be interested as well. Besides having varied, approved curricula, we also need to make sure we have a wide range of different kinds of groups available. Here are some of the questions we ask ourselves to make sure our groups are balanced and well rounded:

- Do we have women's groups?
- Do we have men's groups?
- Do we have married couples' groups?
- Do we have moms' groups?
- Do we have athletic groups?
- Do we have professionals' groups?
- Do we have any age-graded groups (college, 20s, 65+, etc.)?
- Do we have artists' groups?
- Do we have community service-related groups?
- Do we have enough diversity in time and location?

- Do we have enough of these different types of groups, but not too many?
- Are the majority of our groups conveniently timed and located for the majority of our people?

Coaches and team leaders can be very helpful in making sure you have specific types of groups available. For example, if you have a coach or team leader who is passionate about men's ministry, ask him to ensure that at least two to three of the groups on his team are targeted toward men. He will be able to help you identify possible men's group leaders and can take the responsibility of asking those people to lead. Let your coaches and team leaders connect with the group types they are interested in as you think through the different types of groups you'll offer. Also, don't try to get too cute when deciding on your specific group types. Here are three good rules to abide by.

1. *Don't qualify groups with more than one description.* Women's groups are great. Community service groups are great. But you will run into trouble if you offer women's community service groups. Why? The more you qualify, the more you limit your pool of potential group members.

2. *Don't offer too many of one type of group.* One semester we had too many groups for artists (singers, dancers, musicians, designers, etc.). We do have a lot of artists in our church, but not enough to fill up all of the groups that we formed. We seemed to forget, too, that not every artist will sign up for an artists' group. So we quickly turned some of the artists' groups into general groups. As soon as we opened up the groups to a wider pool, our sign-ups increased. We often see churches make a similar mistake when it comes to singles' groups. You do not need to provide a singles' group for

every type of single adult in your church. Some will want to join a general group, a professional group, a women's group or another type of group.

3. *Set goals for the types of groups you would like to have.* The types of groups can include groups that are just for men, women or singles. They could also be more specific, such as groups that are just for runners. Look at your database or the primary interests of those in your church. Again, goal setting is key. Who do you want to target? Set goals for your group types.

A good structure doesn't have to be complicated. In fact, the best structures are the most simple. Your focus is not to build a complicated structure that will impress others but to find a structure that will perfectly complement who you are as a church.

Focus Step #5: Build Your List

The final aspect of Focusing your groups for the upcoming semester is the creation of a list of potential small groups leaders. You can't start forming your groups until you've formulated this list. Using the names you write down, you, your staff coaches and your team leaders will begin the process of asking people to lead. So, before your staff comes together for your small groups Focus meeting, have everyone do some research and come prepared with a list of potential people to contact. If you are the only staff person involved with small groups at this point, you will need to put together the initial list of potential leaders yourself.

Even if you are a small groups lone ranger for the time being, don't hold the Focus meeting without inviting a couple of staff people or a few committed lay people to be involved. You need others to help you prayerfully evaluate previous semesters and set your goals. Plus, you need key people to help you confirm your potential group leaders. They may know something—positive or negative—about a potential leader that you don't know. If you insist on doing your five aspects of Focusing alone (especially the list creation), you'll end up paying for it with sub-par small groups experiences.

Creating a List of Names

So where do you start? How in the world do you pull together a potential list of small groups leaders? First of all, go back and pull the names of every small-group leader or coordinator who has served at any point over the last three semesters. If you are working with staff coaches, they can look back through their teams and form these lists. Review their lists, remove the duplicates and take off anyone who has moved away, left the church or who you just aren't comfortable having lead again.

Next, add any potential new leaders who come to mind. Consider those who have turned down the opportunity to lead a group in the past, but who may be open to leading this semester. Consider people who your current small groups leaders would recommend as good potential leaders from within their groups. Think of involved church members you've met who have never stepped up to lead. The list you formulate during this process should contain far more names than you will actually need to hit your group leaders goal. Remember, not everyone will say yes. At this point, make your "ask list" as long and complete as possible.

At your Focus meeting, let each coach or staff person talk through the list that they brought in. Go over every person they are planning to ask, one by one. Allow for open discussion and ask the following types of questions:

- Did this person do a good job in a previous semester?
- Is there a viable reason to remove this person from the list?

- Is this person involved in a sin that would disqualify him/her from leading?
- Is this person in any way disengaged or disgruntled?
- Do we need to make a phone call to this person before asking him/her to lead, just to make sure everything is okay?
- Does this person need a co-leader?

A note of caution: Don't let the same name end up on more than one coach's list. You don't want an individual asked to lead by multiple staff, in different areas. For example, if someone who has led a general group in the past is now involved on the vocal team, both the worship arts pastor and the general groups coach may want to ask that person to lead a group. Figure out who is going to ask him or her to lead during your Focus meeting, and make sure he or she doesn't get phone calls from both. Not only would that be annoying to the potential group leader, but it would also look as if different staff people were competing over him or her. Use your Focus meeting to iron out these kinds of issues.

If you need yet another reason to talk through your list person by person, think about this: You need to identify those people who never take a break from leading. Leaders need a semester off. They need to be released from leadership service in order to stay effective in the future. We recommend that group leaders serve two semesters a year and then just participate in a group the third semester. But even if you make the "two on and one off" goal clear to your leaders, you will still have some who insist on signing up to lead every semester. Don't let them. You may be tempted to let this slide, especially if you need leaders. But look at the bigger picture: You don't want to burn out your best.

Now that you have your list of potential leaders to contact, you need to do two things. First, *pray for every person on your list*. You will be asking these people to serve as shepherds in your church. So pray for God's guidance as you finalize the list and as you prepare to ask them to lead.

Ask God to prepare their hearts for the task that He may be calling them to. Second, *combine all of your coach/staff lists into one master list.* Finalize all edits and additions to this list. You will give this master list to your coaches and team leaders during the Form month so that they can begin making calls and asking people to lead.

Team Leader Meeting

Now that your Focus meeting is over, and you have a clear picture of what next semester's small groups are going to be, you need to have a meeting with all of your team leaders. At The Journey, the team leaders' meeting always marks the transition from our Focus month to our Form month. If you aren't yet to the stage of having team leaders serve with you, your transition to the Form month will begin just after you finalize your list of names.

Team leaders' meetings are arguably the most important meetings we have all year. We use these meetings to share all of the goals, dates and plans for the upcoming semester with our team leaders. We also take advantage of the time to divide our master list among our team leaders, giving them a list of people to contact within a certain time frame—usually two weeks. We will dive into the details of this meeting in the next section (Form). At this point, just be aware that your master list of names may continue to grow at this meeting. You will want to ask your team leaders if they have other people in mind who would make strong leaders. If the answer is yes, and those people meet all of your criteria, add them to the list. Your list will continue to grow into the Form month, as your current group leaders begin recommending new potential leaders from their current groups.

Team leaders are crucial to the small groups system. We take them very seriously. When we ask someone to serve as a team leader, we are deciding to make a significant investment in him or her through monthly meetings and training resources. We expect team leaders to be faithful in their attendance, serving and tithing, and we ask them to give us permission to hold them accountable in those areas. Team leaders are becoming leaders in the church, so we don't ask just anyone to take on the responsibility. We spend some time in the Focus meeting discussing the best candidates and deciding who we will ask to step up. We only consider Journey members who have served faithfully as a small-group leader in the past.

Once you've decided on your new, potential team leaders, set up a one-on-one meeting with each candidate. Use this time to detail the requirements and responsibilities of being a team leader. Ask them to sign a team leader covenant solidifying those commitments. And never, ever ask them to serve without providing a timeline for their service. At The Journey, we ask our team leaders to serve for one year (or 3 semesters). At the end of that year, they can continue on, but not without signing the covenant again and recommitting to the expectations. The yearly recommitment gives you and your team leaders a natural opportunity to end your agreement if something isn't working. If all is well, it gives them a chance to review their responsibilities and make a fresh commitment to their important role.

Activate Principle
Never ask someone to serve in any area of leadership without providing a beginning and end date for that service.

As the old saying goes, 1 hour of planning will save 10 hours in implementation. How true this is when it comes to the Focus element of your small groups. Your church will never reach its full potential if you aren't willing to take some action and put in the work necessary to plan successful, effective small groups. Always take the time to Focus!

Forming Your Groups

Form

*As Jesus was walking beside the Sea of Galilee, he saw
two brothers, Simon called Peter and his brother Andrew.
They were casting a net into the lake, for they were fishermen.
"Come, follow me," Jesus said, "and I will make you fishers of men."
At once they left their nets and followed him.*

MATTHEW 4:18-20, *NIV*

Congratulations! You have Focused your small groups. You have goals
nailed down and plans in place to accomplish those goals. Now you
must start "seeing the goals" in your own mind so that you can truly
achieve the goals. The second of our Four *F*s will allow you to literally
"see the reaching." As you begin to *Form* your small groups, you will wit-
ness the initial coming together of all the plans and goals you so excit-
edly sketched out during your Focus time. By recruiting and confirming
your group leaders, and getting everything in place for people to actually sign up for your groups, you will be Forming the boundaries of what
is about to become a successful, effective small groups semester.

Let's start by taking a look at the end. How will you know when
you have completed the Form stage, and are ready to move on to the
Fill stage? You have done the Forming you need to do when you have
confirmed the right number of groups for your upcoming semester
and you know all of the information necessary for listing each of those
groups in the catalog and online. This is simple, but not as easy as it

sounds. To officially consider any single group Formed, you need to verify and approve answers to all of the following questions:

1. Who is the leader of the group? Is there a co-leader? Is there a coordinator?
2. What is the topic/study? Book or video series? What appealing blurb will we use in the catalog and online to promote this topic/study?
3. Where will the group meet (this is a general location, not specific address)?
4. What day will the group meet?
5. What time will the group meet?

If you have not confirmed and approved all of this basic information, you cannot consider a group ready to take sign-ups.

You will have three Form months every year. At The Journey, our Form months are April, August and December. Your Form months should be scheduled for the final month of your current groups semester, which will be two months before the next semester is set to begin. For example, if your summer semester kicked off in June and you are preparing for your fall semester, which is set to begin in October, August would be your Form month. In August, your summer groups would be in their last month together, and you would be two months ahead of your fall kick off. Why is this the perfect time? Because prospective group leaders respond better to your invitation to lead if you ask them while the current semester is still in session.

There are two main factors that play into this truth. First, since groups are still meeting, you'll have an easier time communicating with current group leaders about leading again next semester and get better responses when you ask them who in their active group might make a good leader. Second, if you wait until the current semester ends to ask for next semester, you will run into a time crunch. You won't have enough time to both Form and Fill new groups before the next semester begins.

While you will have specific months set aside to Form your groups, the work of this *F* can be much more fluid than the others. You should have an eye out for new leaders throughout the year, not only when your groups are Forming. Say that you have a conversation with someone at a random time during the year, and the person says, "I have always wanted to lead a group but I've been so busy with work. I think I should be able to lead next fall." Plan on it. Mark them down and follow up during your Form month for the fall semester.

Even after you have begun the process of Filling groups for your upcoming semester, be on the lookout to Form new groups. At The Journey, we are often still Forming groups (especially when it comes to confirming information) after group sign-ups have begun, which is technically into the Fill month. From experience, we have found that group leaders who jump in a little late can still have full, successful groups. This may mean that their groups don't make it into the catalog or get listed online for the first couple of weeks, but that usually doesn't hurt them. Just make sure that you update your catalog and webpage week to week. Still, don't add groups too late in the process. Try to contain straggling confirmations to the first couple of weeks. Work hard to get all of your groups Formed by the end of your Form month, but you can take some pressure off by knowing that you do have a little leeway.

Form Step #1: Make the Big Ask

Keep on asking, and you will be given what you ask for. Keep on looking, and you will find. Keep on knocking, and the door will be opened.
JESUS (MATTHEW 7:7)

If you did a thorough Focus job for your upcoming semester by evaluating previous successes and failures, putting the important group dates on your calendar, setting your primary group goals, preparing the semester's structure and creating your initial group leaders ask list, you should be in good shape to begin to Form your groups. Your ability to do this depends on your ability to ask the right people to lead in the right way.

Activate Principle

The Form month is mostly about making the right "asks" of the right people in the right way.

Unfortunately, too many of us put in the hard work of the Focus month only to blow it in the Form month. Why? Usually because we don't know how to make "The Big Ask." Either we are afraid to ask potential group leaders to lead, or we simply don't know how to ask in the right way. Here are three important principles for making the right kind of Big Ask:

Big Ask Principle #1
If you don't ask, you won't receive.
In the Sermon on the Mount, Jesus teaches us to keep on asking, keep on knocking and keep on looking. Persistence, with the right heart, is key. People who are persistent in asking, knocking and looking are usually rewarded. They receive what they have been asking for. Jesus is teaching us that we need to be persistent and not be afraid to approach Him with our bold requests. He is telling us to ask and keep on asking.

In the same way, we have to be bold in asking people in our church to serve as group leaders. So often the fear of rejection makes us timid. We don't want to bother anyone, inconvenience anyone or have anyone tell us no. Can we be bold with you? *Get over it.* Learning to be an effective leader is directly linked to learning to ask people to do what you need them to do. What's the worst thing that can happen? They might say no. Big deal. Maybe they will think about it and lead next time around because you were bold enough to ask this time. Anyway, you have an entire list of people who would make great leaders.

Think about the best thing that can happen: You ask, they say yes and they go on to lead a thriving group in which people grow closer to God, deeper in their relationships with each other and experience life-change. Did you notice the first part of that list? "You ask." How can we let our fear block the blessing that God wants to bring? If you don't ask people to lead, most of them will never step up and volunteer on their own initiative. You have been called to this work. Making the Big Ask is your job. Don't let the enemy's tool of fear back you down.

Just as you have to have the courage to make the Big Ask of each potential group leader, you also need to be humble enough to make the Big Ask of God. Before you begin this process, ask God for His favor in recruiting group leaders. Ask Him to take away your fear of asking, if you struggle with that. Ask Him for wisdom on who and how to ask, and trust Him to provide the right group leaders. Each time you pick up the phone, ask God to prepare the heart of the person on the other end to receive your call. This is not about you. God has a work to accomplish here and you are His tool. So ask Him to use you in the most effective way possible.

Big Ask Principle #2
Leading a group is not an obligation . . . it is an opportunity.
Another mistake we often make in asking someone to lead a group is to turn our asking into an apology. We make it seem as if, by leading a group, a person will be doing us a personal favor ("Can you help me out?"), taking on a heavy burden ("It will only be an inconvenience for a few months"), or fulfilling a spiritual obligation ("We need you to do this to help the church"). First of all, asking in this way will get you turned down more times than not. Second, even if you do get the individual to

lead a group, it's doubtful he or she will approach the semester in a positive state of mind. When you ask someone to lead a group, you are not asking that person to help you out; you are offering the opportunity to embark on a spiritual adventure, to make a difference, to engage in what God created them to do. It's not an obligation; it's an opportunity to have eternal influence!

Think about how Jesus made the Big Ask of Peter and James when He wanted them to become His disciples (see Matt. 4:19). He didn't say, "Hey, guys, I understand you may not want to or you may be too busy, but I was wondering if you might possibly consider maybe helping me out. If not, that's okay. Sorry again for bothering you." No. Instead, Jesus asked boldly. He said, "Come, be my disciples, and I will show you how to fish for people!" Come, follow Me—not because it's an obligation, but because it's a tremendous opportunity for you to do something big. That's why we like to call this "The Big Ask." You are truly asking people to do something big—bigger than anything else they do.

Jesus did not apologize for asking Peter and James, or anyone for that matter, to follow Him. To the contrary, He clearly presented becoming His follower as a tremendous privilege and opportunity to be involved in something with eternal significance. See the connection? We are still asking people to follow Jesus in making disciples. Most people are struggling to find significance, meaning and purpose in what they do every day. When we have the chance to add value to their lives—to challenge them to be a part of something that might change eternity—we should never apologize for it. Instead of being in any way timid or apologetic, we need to approach potential leaders as if we are giving them an incredible gift. And that is exactly what we are doing! Can you imagine what would happen if we began asking people to lead groups from this perspective?

Make the Big Ask with your focus on opportunity over obligation. An incredible illustration of this truth's power is the famous account of how Steve Jobs (founder of Apple) convinced John Sculley (the head of

Pepsi-Co) to leave Pepsi and join his organization. In the mid 1980s, Steve asked John simply, "Do you want to sell sugared water all your life or do you want to change the world?" Of course, the former Pepsi executive chose the latter. Although the pairing ultimately failed to work out, the story shows that when people understand that they are being given an opportunity to do something that matters, it doesn't matter how busy they are or how intimidating the task may be . . . they will say yes with enthusiasm.

So before you apologize for asking someone to serve as a group leader, ask yourself, *Is there anything I have to apologize for? Am I putting this person in a position to fail? Am I asking them to do something that will clutter their lives and doesn't matter?* If so, don't make the ask. But if there is something worthwhile going on and you are inviting them to be a part of it, you ought to be jumping out of your seat to ask them to join you in changing the world through leading a group at your church.

Big Ask Principle #3:
Asking people to lead helps them climb the leadership ladder.
At The Journey, we've established an imaginary leadership ladder. No one comes to our church and steps into a key leadership position at the top of the ladder. No matter how long you have been a follower of Jesus, how mature you are in your faith or how impressive your reputation, you have to climb the leadership ladder step by step beginning with an entry-level service position. If you are faithful in the smaller things, you are then given more and more responsibility in the larger things. Doesn't the Bible say that somewhere?!

Like most churches, we have a large pool of people attending The Journey who are not involved. They like to hang out on the periphery. In an effort to connect those people on a deeper level, we want to get as many of them as possible serving in some area. As they begin to serve, we can identify the leaders and help them climb the leadership ladder. Each rung brings more responsibility and more accountability.

As you Form your groups, keep in mind that small groups are one of the best engines for leadership development. They catalyze growth. They provide an ideal environment for recognizing potential leaders and they are filled with built-in opportunities to climb to the ladder's next rung. When you ask people to step out of their comfort zone and take on some responsibility, you are giving them an opportunity for spiritual, emotional and relational development. If you allow them to continue hanging out on the edges of your church's action, they won't grow. We don't grow when we are comfortable. Get excited about challenging your people to step out of their comfort zone and into an area of ministry that forces their growth and development. Both of you will benefit greatly in the long run.

At The Journey, leading a group is not the first rung on the leadership ladder. That first step might be serving at a Sunday service or at the office during the week. Or it may be participating in an outreach project or just being in a group and assisting the leader. But we also make sure that being a group leader is not one of the last steps on the ladder. We don't set the bar so high that only a few can do it. We try to make leading a group uncomplicated and manageable for ordinary people.

Setting the Bar

When Jesus asked Peter and James to follow Him in Matthew 4, His request was simple and straightforward: "Follow Me." No heavy-handed requirements. No spiritual litmus test. And He wasn't asking biblical scholars or religious giants to follow Him. They were ordinary men, commercial fishermen. (Later on, Jesus would ask some characters to follow Him who were even more iffy.) Jesus did not set the bar for discipleship so high that it excluded average people. All He was interested in was the condition of the heart.

In Big Idea #4, we learned that your group leaders should be apprentices, not experts. This mindset gives you the freedom to raise up new leaders in the same way that Jesus did (and the same way that Paul did). Remember how Paul would leave his churches in the hands of relatively new believers? If Jesus could trust a couple of fishermen to be His disciples and Paul could trust inexperienced believers to oversee the ministry and teaching of new churches, surely we can trust our followers of Jesus with our small groups even if they are average people.

Don't set the bar too high for being a group leader. Instead, use group leadership as an opportunity to challenge someone who has been hiding in his or her comfort zone to take a step up on the leadership ladder. Ironically, many of the best group leaders we've had at The Journey have been people we were initially hesitant to ask. And many of those who seemed to be the most qualified (i.e., had the most biblical knowledge) were some of the worst. After years of analyzing who makes a good group leader and who doesn't, here again is our list of requirements for the potential group leader:

- A follower of Jesus
- Attends The Journey faithfully
- Has been in a group before, preferably as a coordinator
- Recommended by a group leader, member or staff person
- On track to become a member (though not ideal, a person can lead his or her first group without becoming a member of the church but must take the step of membership before leading multiple times)

Although it is not required, we want new group leaders to have served as a group coordinator in at least one previous group. Service as a group coordinator is a great way for someone to begin climbing the leadership ladder. Often, group leaders will identify potential coordinators from their previous groups and invite them to be their coordinator in an upcoming group. Sometimes a group will begin without an official coordinator in place. But the group leader will then recognize leadership potential in a group member and ask him or her to serve as coordinator for the rest of the semester, which puts the member up a rung and starts hands-on leadership training.

Becoming a group leader at The Journey was much tougher in the early days. During the first year-and-a-half of our church, prospective leaders had to complete a small-group leader application, have a one-on-one interview with a pastor, and attend our three-hour membership class (if they weren't already members); this in addition to our required half-day Small-Group Leader Training. Then one semester, just after our church had gone through a growth spurt, we realized that something had to change. We saw that we could either have too few groups the next semester, all equipped with "qualified" leaders, or we could lower our incredibly high bar and have enough groups to serve all of the people God was sending us. The decision was a no-brainer. We restructured our group leader requirements. We stopped expecting more of our leaders than Jesus expected of His disciples, and we learned an important lesson—to trust God with our leaders and to trust our leaders with our groups!

Activate Principle
Trust God with your leaders and trust your
leaders with your groups.

Your best initial source of potential leaders will be those individuals who are currently leading groups. Besides asking them directly, one way to keep your current group leaders' minds focused on the idea of leading again and raising up new leaders is through the weekly update email (see Facilitate) that goes out to small-group leaders. At least once during your Form month, send an email update and ask group leaders to reply to two quick questions: (1) *Will I lead a small group next semester?* and (2) *Who in my current group would be a good group leader?*

Not only is this an effective way for a team leader or coach to contact current group leaders about leading again, but it also reinforces that initial contact through weekly updates. (For examples of several "Small-Group Leaders Updates," visit www.ActivateBook.com.)

Your Calendar and the Big Ask

Before you start asking people to be group leaders, take time to review the calendar you created during your Focus month. You should have the following dates marked:

1. The date when the initial asks begin
2. The date by which initial asks should be completed
3. The date by which follow-up calls should be made and follow-up emails sent to prospective leaders
4. The date by which you want groups confirmed
5. The last possible date on which a group can be confirmed and still be included in the first-week catalog and webpage

Here is a partial calendar example from The Journey. This calendar is for the Form month for our fall semester:

- **Monday, July 16:** Team leader meeting. All team leaders receive lists of potential group leaders to contact. (Still in Focus month.)

- **Wednesday, August 1:** Deadline for all initial asks. By this date, everyone on the master list should have been contacted at least once about the possibility of leading a group. (Note that we allowed about two weeks for initial asks before the official Form month even began.) At The Journey, team leaders, coaches and staff will all help with initial asks. But from this point forward, the coaches will take charge and begin following up to confirm groups for their own teams.

- **Wednesday, August 15:** Deadline for confirmations. By this date, you need to know who is leading, but you don't yet have to have all of the day/time/location/study details confirmed. You can still confirm leaders after the deadline, but having it in place provides your team with structure and a sense of urgency.

- **Wednesday, August 29:** Deadline for details. You need to know the day/time/location/study details for all of your groups by this date in order to get them listed in the catalog and online for the first week of sign-ups. Sign-ups begin the first Sunday in September (start of Fill month). As mentioned, you can continue to Form new groups and confirm leaders for a few weeks into the Fill month.

Goals are just dreams with deadlines. If you don't set aggressive deadlines for your Form month, that is what your group goals will turn into—just dreams. Mark your deadlines on the calendar each semester and stick to them!

Form Step #2: Schedule the Team Leader Meeting

Let's jump back to the team leader meeting that we discussed briefly at the end of the Focus section. This meeting will mark your transition from the Focus month to the Form month. As we mentioned, you'll want to schedule it for about two weeks before your official Form month begins. When you bring all of your team leaders together, it's time to lay out your plan for the coming semester and get them ready to start making asks by doing three things.

Share the Ask List

Give your team leaders the list of potential group leaders you want them to contact about leading. Make sure you include phone numbers and addresses on the list, and emphasize the deadline for initial asks. Also try to have 10-plus potential leaders on each team leader's list, since you want them to confirm five groups. At The Journey, we usually allow team leaders two to three weeks to make asks. Once they've finished, they meet with their coaches to review how it went. From this point on, coaches do most of the follow-up and final confirmation. (Team leaders help when possible.)

Note that team leaders are not just haphazardly given potential group leader names. If possible, fill each team leader's list with the names of people who have served on his or her team in the past or who he or she knows personally. Building a level of familiarity into the ask will go a long way. Keeping teams together for multiple semesters also helps nurture existing relationships between team leaders and group leaders, clearing the way for shepherding and pastoral care throughout the semester and beyond. Of course, many of the names will be new, but do what you can.

Get Feedback

Rather than simply hand your team leaders a list of names to call, get their feedback on each potential group leader on that list. Listen to your team leaders. They may know something about a potential leader that you don't know. Also ask if there's anyone to add to the list. They will almost always think of potential leaders you may have overlooked or that you may not even know yet. After you've made changes from their feedback, make sure your team leaders understand what they are supposed to do and by what date.

Talk About How to Make the Big Ask

Finally, and perhaps most important, review how to make the Big Ask. Cover this process every semester, no matter how many times you, the staff coaches or the team leaders have asked people to lead groups. Everyone needs encouragement to "keep on asking." At The Journey, we actually have a handout that spells out exactly what to do when contacting a potential group leader.

Making the Big ASK

ASK how the potential Group Leader/Coordinator is doing personally and how the current group is going (if he or she is currently leading one). *Remember, one of your primary responsibilities is to provide support and spiritual leadership.*

ASK if he or she would like to lead a group during the upcoming semester. Be prepared to share details about the upcoming semester, such as important dates. *Be encouraging and supportive. Don't use the word "need," but let the person know that you want him or her to lead.*

What if he or she says, "Yes, I would like to lead"? *Show excitement and give encouragement. After the confirmation:*

- Give the date/time for the upcoming Growth Group Leaders Training (it's required).

- Confirm as many of the details about the group as you can (day, time, location, study, group type, co-leader, coordinator).

What if the person says, "No, I don't want to lead"?

- If the person just wants to take the semester off, thank him or her and let that person know you will be in touch next semester to invite him or her to lead again.

- If the person never wants to lead again, find out what the issue is, offer assistance and, if necessary, ask if he or she would like to talk with a pastor. Always be encouraging and supportive of the person's service.

What if the person says "maybe"?

- Do your best to honestly alleviate any fears the person has about leading. Suggest a co-leader or coordinator to assist.

- Suggest attractive options for kinds of groups the person might want to lead (ask your Coach).

- Let him or her know that you will be praying and will be in touch next week.

In all cases, be appreciative and let your coach know ASAP! Then ASK the person if there is anyone in his or her current Growth Group that he or she would recommend as a Leader or Coordinator for the upcoming semester. *You may have to encourage the person to think about someone. Be sure to share the names of those potential leaders with your Coach before asking anyone new.*

ASK the person if there is anything you can do for him or her or if there is a specific way you can be praying for him or her. Say "thank you." *Make sure the person knows that you want to serve him or her in any way you can.*

FOLLOW UP with the new names of potential leaders you were given during your conversation. First let your coach know, and then follow the same process as above with them. Hopefully, every current group will have at least one recommendation for a new small-group leader. *Be ready to suggest the topics/studies that your coach recommends. Keep your coach updated throughout the process.*

Follow up regularly with your team leaders and all those who are responsible for asking people to lead groups. Don't take for granted that everything you ask them to do will happen, especially when working with volunteers. Make sure you always know exactly where you stand with regard to getting your groups confirmed and reaching your goals.

Form Step #3: Get Your Groups List Ready

A group is not fully formed just because you have confirmed a leader. You have to get a group ready to be listed for sign-ups. Here's what you need to do to get your groups list ready:

1. *Confirm that the leader is committed.*

2. *Determine if there will be a co-leader or coordinator* helping with the group. Many times someone who agrees to lead a group has not even thought about the possibility of having someone to assist. Find out if there is someone the leader knows who may like to lead with him or her or serve as the coordinator.

3. *Confirm the group's day, time and general location.* The earlier you know this information, the better understanding you will have of how all the groups are balancing each other. As far as location, we've learned never to list the exact address of a group in the catalog or online. Instead, list the general area. The group leader can give the specific address to group members as they sign up. Make sure you safeguard this level of protection for your leaders.

4. *Determine the type of group.* Will this be a general group or a men's group? An artists' group or a moms' group? Or will the group be sports oriented or community service oriented? Nail it down.

5. *Confirm the book/topic the group will be studying.* Obviously, you get a pass on this one during church-wide campaign semesters. But for the semesters when group leaders choose their own curriculum, try to get a decision on this as early as possible. Deciding what topic to focus on can be a difficult decision for new leaders. Urge them along and remember your responsibility in making sure that the curriculum they choose is strong and theologically sound.

6. *Finalize a two- to three-sentence blurb about the group.* You can use some of the language from the back cover of the book being studied. This blurb will appear in your catalog and online next to the group listing. It should be upbeat and make people want to join. If you can, put a link on your website next to each group listing that will take the person signing up to Amazon.com (or wherever else they can buy the book/study immediately). When signing up online, you want people to be able to sign up and purchase the book in a matter of minutes.

Communicate with Your Confirmed Leaders

While you are in the process of collecting all of this information from your confirmed leaders, use the opportunity to communicate some important details to them. Make sure your leaders know the following:

1. The Date and Time for Small-Group Leader Training

All leaders are required to attend this training no matter how many groups they've led in the past. If they absolutely cannot attend, they must make up the training by listening to it on CD or meeting personally with a staff person. We will talk more about what this training looks like in the Facilitate section.

2. Semester Start and End Dates

The start week is the same for every group, even though some groups might have a curriculum that is shorter or longer than others. All groups should last 10 to 12 weeks.

3. The Art of Syllabus Creation

Well, it's not an art really, but it is a necessity. All group leaders are required to put together a staff-approved syllabus for their group. The syllabus simply lists meeting dates and indicates what material will be covered each week (usually by providing a weekly reading schedule). For a sample group syllabus, see www.ActivateBook.com.

4. The Date and Time for the Next Membership Class

Invite group leaders who are not yet members to sign up for the next membership class. Those who decide they do not want to become members within a semester or two after leading their first group will not be asked to lead again.

The Mid-Month Evaluation Meeting

As the old military saying goes, "No battle plan ever survives first contact with the enemy." In the same way, the plans and goals you laid out so carefully during your Focus month will invariably need to be altered and re-evaluated as your Fill month nears. Don't be caught off guard. Schedule a mid-Form-month evaluation meeting to check up on yourself. Pull your team together and look at how well you are reaching your goals. Are the number of groups on track? Are the types of groups you wanted shaping up? If we may say it again, evaluation is the key to excellence.

At The Journey, we have a group strategy meeting every week, when we examine our reality versus our goals. You don't have to do it every week (though it probably wouldn't be a bad idea), but be sure that you plan at least one assessment meeting no later than halfway through the month. Use the meeting to ask yourself and your team the following questions:

1. Are we on schedule to have enough groups?
2. Are we going to have too many?
3. What adjustments or changes do we need to make to our strategy in order to be successful?
4. Do we still need to find leaders?
5. Do we need to combine some existing leaders to make their groups stronger?

A note on number 5: Whether you plan it from the beginning or see the need during your evaluation, be creative in pairing co-leaders to form new groups. For example, you might pair a businessperson who has led several times in the past with a new leader who is a little bit inexperienced but is eager to serve. Pair good friends who might be nervous about leading for the first time but who feel much more comfortable when given the opportunity to lead with someone they trust. Putting co-leaders together isn't a science. A little finesse is required. But when you get the hang of creatively pairing potential leaders, you are able to form exciting, thriving groups that may have otherwise been impossible.

Now that you have the number of groups you need, and you have all of the information for those groups nailed down, your groups are officially *fully formed*! On to the next step. Time to Fill those groups with eager members!

Filling Your Groups

Fill

[They met] day after day, in the temple courts and from house to house.
ACTS 5:42, *NIV* (EMPHASIS ADDED)

You have your leaders in place, you have your curriculum chosen, and you have your catalog ready to go. You have it all, except for one thing: people in the groups! At this point, maybe you feel a little bit like the professor who said, "This University would be a wonderful place if it weren't for all the students!" The professor missed the point of the university. It exists for the students. The same is true with groups. Everything we have done so far has been preparation for this stage of the game—getting people into groups.

If no one joins the groups you have focused and formed, then your efforts have been in vain. There will be no life-change, no discipleship, no friendships. Nothing happens until people sign up and show up for your groups. This is a critical juncture. Fortunately, there are 11 proven methods to fill your groups. But before we get to those, let's (1) revisit our calendar, (2) revisit the goal you set for group sign-ups in the Focus section, and (3) examine the promotion month in more detail.

Calendar: Fill Months

As you know by now, in the semester system there are three Fill months a year, also referred to as promotion months. For many churches, Fill months will be January, May and September. Perhaps you defined your

Fill months earlier but not the exact dates. Let's do that now. Grab your calendar and decide which promotion month you are working on and let's get detailed about it. Here are a few questions to ask:

1. *What date will group sign-ups begin for the upcoming semester?* This date should have been determined, since it was the driving force behind forming your groups, but it never hurts to revisit. This date is usually a Sunday, and it's the first day the groups catalog is published.

2. *When will online sign-ups be available?* (More on online sign-ups below.)

3. *How many Sundays will we push group sign-ups?*

4. *What are the newsletter deadlines for getting group sign-ups listed?* (More on using a newsletter to drive group sign-ups below.)

5. *What is the last day someone can sign up for a group this semester?*

Here's an example of a recent Journey promotion month calendar:

January 7 (Sunday)
No formal mention of groups from the stage unless teaching pastor decides to include it. Possible announcement in the program that group sign-ups will begin on January 21. Anyone who indicates an interest in groups on the back of their Connection Card will be contacted and made aware that group sign-ups begin January 21.

January 9
Group Coaches Meeting
Final prep for sign-ups

January 14 (Sunday)
Same as January 7

January 19-20 (Friday/Saturday)
Group Team Leaders Retreat

January 21 (Sunday)
Signups begin at the service and online. Every attender will receive a groups catalog with their program. A few group leaders will staff a table in the lobby before and after each service to display curriculum, answer questions and, most important, sign up members. From the stage, people are invited to sign up for a group in one of three ways: (1) on the website, (2) on the Connection Card, or (3) at the groups table in the lobby.

January 22 (Monday)
Follow up with everyone who signed up for a group yesterday. This happens every Monday from now through late February. Follow-up continues throughout the week, as online sign-ups are received.

January 23 (Tuesday)
Promote groups in the newsletter, starting today and continuing through late February.

January 27 (Saturday)
Group Leaders Training

January 28 (Sunday)
Group sign-ups continue. Teaching pastor integrates push for groups into the Sunday message.

January 31 (Wednesday)
Groups pastor follows up with everyone from previous semester who is not yet signed up for a group.

February 4 (Sunday)
New teaching series begins with a Big Day in the church. (For more on utilizing Big Days in your church to spur groups and evangelism, see

www.ActivateBook.com.) Give groups major emphasis through a drama, a video or a testimony. Ask group leaders to stand in the service, recognize them and pray for them.

February 7 (Wednesday)
Everyone in the church's database who is not in a group receives an invitation to join a group from either the lead pastor or the groups pastor.

February 11 (Sunday)
Distribute a catalog of remaining groups with the program. Ask everyone signed up for a group to raise their hand in the service. Make a final push for sign-ups.

February 12 (Monday)
Groups begin meeting weekly.

February 18 (Sunday) to March 4 (Sunday)
Continue group sign-ups for open groups (i.e., groups that aren't full).

The Fill process actually lasts almost two months because of its overlap with the beginning of groups. It is normal for one or two of your promotion months to be longer than the others. We find that our spring and fall promotion months are usually a bit longer than our summer promotion month. Let the teaching calendar and the length of your semesters determine how long you Fill. Even though your sign-ups may continue for six or seven straight weeks, the force of your push should be in the three or four weeks leading up to the semester's kick off.

Sign-Up Goal

We believe that goal setting is a godly activity—a veritable act of faith. We've even been known to argue that a modern application of Matthew 9:29 could read, "According to your goals will it be done unto you."

Think about it. You have no idea how many people will join your newly created groups, but on faith you are setting a goal in expectation of what God might do in your church. Goals are an outward expression of what you are trusting God to accomplish.

To clarify, our sign-up goal is exactly that—a hopeful estimation of the number of people who will sign up for a small group. Perhaps you are wondering why we set a sign-up goal instead of a show-up goal. Sign-ups are simply an important gauge. We know for sure that sign-ups affect show-ups, and if we want more people to show up for our groups, then we must have more people sign up. Sign-ups are also easier to track from one semester to the next.

In the Facilitate section, we will talk about how to determine the number of sign-ups versus the number of show-ups. Since more people will sign up than show up for groups, it is important that we set an appropriately high goal. As the artist Michelangelo said one time, "The greater danger for most of us lies not in setting our aim too high and falling short; but in setting our aim too low, and achieving our mark." What is your sign-ups goal for your upcoming semester—the one you set during your Focus month? Write it here:

_____

_____

_____

_____

_____

Does this number force you to have faith? If not, it may be too small. Does it seem utterly out of reach? Then perhaps it's too large. If your goal forces you to trust God but doesn't seem completely out of the realm of possibility, then you may have set just the right goal. In our experience, this is an important number. We've seen how setting this goal for group sign-ups can affect both life-change in our groups and in our church as a whole. Why? Because groups influence every other area of the church. Increased faith in this area will lead to increased faith overall.

Promotion Month

Now that you have your basic Fill calendar and a clear sign-ups goal in place, let's examine the individual elements of filling your groups. The most basic element is the promotion month—the period when you are recruiting, inspiring, pushing, motivating, teaching/preaching and using positive peer pressure to move people to sign up for a group. Make sure that your entire promotion month is dedicated exclusively to getting sign-ups. If anything is competing with group sign-ups, you will see less-than-desired results.

For example, you don't want to have any attention going toward a capital campaign recruitment or a women's retreat during this month. These worthy causes will take attention away from the most important, most pressing initiative: getting people connected in small groups for the coming semester. As strange as it sounds, we've discovered that if people have more than one "sign-up choice" on a Sunday (i.e., to sign up for a group or to sign up for a retreat), they won't sign up for either. You want your people in groups. Joining one should be the only decision in front of them.

Wrangling your people's attention exclusively to small group sign-ups takes discipline. No matter how intense you are about focusing on groups, there will always be competing causes trying to find their way into the mix. You have to be intentional about choosing the "best" over the "good." The other opportunities sneaking in are probably very good, in general, but we guarantee that they will negatively influence your sign-ups, which are "best" for everyone. That women's retreat, while amazing, will be over in a weekend. But if a woman signs up for a small group instead, she will be involved in a life-changing environment for at least a semester, and probably for every semester after. She may even go on to be a leader. Then a team leader. Ultimately, the small groups system will give her a much better opportunity to become a fully developing follower of Jesus than the weekend retreat. That is "best." So, during your promotion month, don't put the option out there. Don't give her the opportunity to relegate best for good. Don't put drag on your own system. Zero in on group sign-ups. You'll be glad you did.

We know how hard this can be, but it is possible. You will have staff members who come to you "needing" to recruit for their projects during the promotion month. We are constantly explaining to our staff and key leaders that, yes, their projects are important—so important that we should wait to recruit for them when it won't compete with small groups. We don't want to do a disservice to either opportunity.

Our worship arts team is a great example. Because of the high number of artists in our church, we hold auditions to be on the worship team. These auditions always fall close to group sign-ups time. While the auditions are not promoted from the main stage, they are promoted in our newsletter, in other printed materials and in the lobby. So we must carefully use the calendar or worship arts and groups would both suffer. Currently, audition sign-ups are held either just before groups sign-ups begin or just after, depending on the semester. Getting worship arts auditions on a different calendar system than groups has allowed both ministries to flourish, whereas putting them on a closely similar schedule would have negatively impacted both. (For more on our worship arts ministries and how they are structured see www. ActivateBook.com.)

Activate Principle
Devote the entire promotion month
exclusively to group sign-ups.

You'll notice that promotion gets more intense as the semester's start date approaches. As the start date for our groups draws closer, our intensity increases each week. Three or four weeks before the start of the semester, we announce that group sign-ups are available and provide a catalog and basic sign-up directions. That's all. When you first start implementing this groups system, you may have to do more on the first day of sign-ups. But after a few strong semesters, the sheer anticipation of new groups will bring you 25 percent to 30 percent of your sign-ups in the first week that sign-ups open.

Here's How It Works

One Month Until Groups Start
Announce that groups are open, hand out catalogs and give clear instructions for how to sign up.

Three Weeks Until Groups Start
Announce that groups are open, hand out catalogs and give clear instructions for how to sign up. Have a few group leaders staff an information table in the lobby, and ask all of your group leaders to stand up in the service. You may also want to give your group leaders special name tags so that they are noticed by attenders. You want everyone to see that your group leaders are normal people, easily known.

Two Weeks Until Groups Start
Announce that groups are open, hand out catalogs and give clear instructions for how to sign up. Have a few group leaders staff an information table in the lobby, and ask all of your group leaders to stand up in the service. Teach a message highlighting the importance of groups. You may want to focus the message around a theme such as loneliness, relationships, finding friendship or spiritual growth. Make sure you hit the groups head-on—no subtlety required. (For more examples and to download transcripts, see www.ActivateBook.com.)

One Week Until Groups Start

Announce that groups are open, hand out catalogs and give clear instructions for how to sign up. Have a few group leaders staff an information table in the lobby, and ask all of your group leaders to stand up in the service. Teach a message that highlights the importance of groups. *Invite everyone who has already joined a group to raise his or her hand during the service. Feature a testimony about a small-group experience or show a groups promotion video. (As a side note, the testimony is always more effective than the video. Don't get so focused on technology that you forget about the power of testimony.)*

The rolling stone builds momentum every week. There are some in your church who will join a group just because they are being offered the opportunity. There are others who will never join a group no matter what you do. But the majority of your people will fall in the middle. They will join a group if you give them a big enough reason to. These are the people you are targeting during the promotion month. Give them a strong enough "why" and they'll be on board. If you let them know why they should sign up, in a creative, emotional and personal way, they'll sign up faster. So think about why your people need to be in a small group. Take a moment now and list the top 10 reasons why someone in your church should sign up:

1. _____

2. _____

3. _____

4. _____

5. _____

6. _____

7. _____

8. _____

9. _____

10. _____

Now ask yourself, *How can I make sure these 10 reasons are incorporated into our promotion month?* Don't just tell them they need to join; show them. Be creative. Use sermons, testimonies, positive peer pressure and fun to spur them to action.

Positive peer pressure has been mentioned several times, so perhaps it's time to explain: When we think of peer pressure, we normally think of the negative pressure our peers put on us to do something we shouldn't do. I (Nelson) experienced negative peer pressure in junior high school when my friends pressured me into staying out past my curfew. When I tried to explain to my mom that *"everyone* was staying out that late," she replied, "If everyone jumped off the Brooklyn Bridge, would you do it too?" Maybe that was an early sign from God that I would spend my life and ministry in New York City!

But peer pressure can also be positive. You may have wondered why we have people who have signed up for a group raise their hands (or sometimes even stand) in the service. Positive peer pressure. Not only does this act affirm and deepen the commitment of those who have already signed up, by making their decision public, but it also serves as positive peer pressure for those who haven't signed up. It causes those hesitant few to say, "Wow! Look at everyone who has signed up. Maybe I should too."

In marketing, it's called the bandwagon effect. "If everyone else is doing it, I should probably jump on the bandwagon." Positive peer pressure can be an effective tool as long as the motives are pure and it is being used to push people to something that will give them a deeper connection with Christ. With full integrity, we can utilize positive peer pressure to accomplish godly goals.

Now, as promised, let's get to the top 11 ways to Fill your newly Formed small groups.

Fill Factor #1: One-Step Sign-Ups

Here's a simple yet profound question for you: How does someone sign up for a group at your church? We've asked hundreds of church leaders that question over the last several years and we've heard some pretty complicated answers to such a simple question. In fact, we've come across many churches who seem to have the whole small groups thing together—full-color catalogs, willing leaders, powerful curriculum and a solid group calendar—yet they can't fill their groups. Why? People don't know how to sign up.

Have you ever heard the expression "Big doors swing on small hinges"? How true that is when it comes to filling your groups! You can do everything else in the world right, but if you don't polish the small hinge of how someone signs up for a group at your church, the door won't swing. From our experience, churches make one of two mistakes.

Mistake #1: Lack of Clarity

People say no to any proposition that is unclear. That's a universal rule. Not long ago, I (Nelson) received a call from a mega-church in California. They asked me if I'd be willing to consult with their groups pastor and help them achieve 100 percent adult participation. The proposal was intriguing but I wasn't sure if I had the time.

I agreed to start with a phone conversation. During the initial conversation, the groups pastor explained that a few weeks earlier they'd had a big push to get people into small groups. They handed out catalogs as people entered the worship service, and the pastor had taught an inspiring message on the importance of being in a group. After the service, they'd held a small groups fair in their gym where every group had a table and anyone interested could ask questions. The day went great, was well attended and appeared to be an overall success except for one problem: less than 10 percent of their people signed up for a group.

As I listened, I recognized that they had done many things right: identified leaders, planned a big day at church, set up a great message on groups, given an opportunity for people to ask questions, announced a clear start date, etc. But they also made some mistakes—a few minor ones and one killer. The minor mistakes included only having sign-ups on one Sunday. I advised that the next time, they needed to have a build-up approach to sign-ups, increasing the focus and intensity each week. Having sign-ups on only one Sunday seriously limited the potential number of people who could commit.

The killer mistake was their sign-up process. I asked the pastor, "If someone wanted to sign up for a group, how did they do it?" He gave me a list of answers: "They could tell one of our leaders, they could tell me or, I guess, they could call our office . . ."

We've made this mistake too. We've taught messages on evangelism but failed to clarify how someone should report their new faith decision. We've challenged people to get in a group but not laid out a clear path for how they could join. Can you imagine?

Activate Principle

People don't join anything if it's unclear how they should do so.

Make it crystal clear how someone signs up for a group at your church. Here are three particularly effective ways.

1. Sign Up During the Sunday Service

Your Sunday service is an ideal place for sign-ups, especially if the pastor is teaching on groups or if you are having another kind of groups push. Let people sign up on the spot, while the sentiment is fresh on their hearts. Our approach has been to give people a sign-up blank on the Connection Card during promotion months. They will be filling out their contact information and any "next steps" they want to take anyway, so we use this opportunity to also get them to commit to a group. (For more information on the power of the Connection Card for assimilation and next steps of faith, see *Fusion: Turning First-Time Guests into Fully Engaged Members of Your Church*.)

MY NEXT STEP TODAY IS TO:

O Memorize Proverbs 7:2-3.

O Read the story of Solomon in 1 Kings 3.

O Accept the One-Year Bible Challenge.

O Find out more about upcoming Play Groups:

    O Friday, Jan. 20: Glory Road Movie Play Group

    O Friday, Jan. 27: Extreme Bowling

SEND ME INFO ABOUT:

O Becoming a follower of Jesus.

O Baptism.

O Growth Groups.

O Church membership.

O Serving @ The Journey.

O Servant Evangelism Saturday.

Sign me up for Growth Group # _____

Comments, Prayer Requests: _____

_____

Calling for a decision at the moment of inspiration is very important. Always allow people the opportunity to respond when God speaks to them. For example, let's say you've just had a church member share a brief testimony on how being in a small group changed his life. After the testimony, the teaching pastor would want to say something like this:

What a powerful story José has just shared. Maybe you know in your heart that you need to be in a group this next semester. Everyone, take out your Connection Card and look at the back. If you are ready to sign up today, just find the number of the group that is right for you in your groups catalog and write that number in the space on the back of your card. That's all you need to do. Later this week, we'll be in touch with more info on the group you selected. Make sure that your name, email address and phone number are on the front of the card. In a few minutes, when we receive our offering, just drop your completed Connection Card in the plate when it's passed.

Giving people a clear path for growth when God is speaking to them is ministry at its best.

2. Offer Sign-ups on Your Website

Most of your people will probably be very comfortable and willing to sign up for a group online. This is an important option to give them, but only after you have maximized your Sunday sign-ups. With the online opportunity, you are simply trying to recreate the Sunday sign-up process on your website. Make sure these key elements are in place:

- A system to drive potential group members toward the website to sign up (We put the website on all printed materials related to group sign-ups and point people to the website with emails and newsletters.)
- A link from your home page to the groups sign-up area
- A clear, easily searched list of available groups
- A simple sign-up form to fill out

Don't try to do too much with your website at first. Start small and improve the functionality with each semester. Once you have these basic elements set, you can slowly develop a more evolved online sign-up system. Our current system sends an automatic welcome email to the person who joins a group, gives them a link to purchase the curriculum, notifies the group leader and our staff of the new sign-up, adds the new member to our database and closes a group when it is full.

When we first started the small groups system at The Journey, the online option was much more rudimentary, and it accounted for less than 10 percent of our sign-ups. Today it is our most popular sign-up method. But remember, mastering Sunday sign-ups is a prerequisite to having a successful online sign-up option. (To learn more about the Web consultants we recommend, visit www.ActivateBook.com.)

3. Sign Up at the Groups Table in the Lobby

Have some of your group leaders staff a table in the lobby after each service during your promotion months. Granted, you'll only get a small percentage of sign-ups this way as compared to the first two options. Nonetheless, the groups table meets a real need for many of your people—those who need a little personal touch before signing up. Maybe they have one key question they need answered, or they don't feel comfortable signing up until they have met some leaders face to face. The groups table is the place where the "almost committed" can take that step of faith and sign on the dotted line. We'll discuss the groups table in more detail in Fill Factor #4.

Mistake #2: Too Many Steps

As we've established, people say no if something is confusing. And making something overly complicated makes it confusing. The more steps involved in a process, the more complicated it appears, even if the steps are easy and obvious. Your goal should be to make signing up for a group as easy, clear and simple as possible. You can do that by establishing *one-step sign-ups*.

Many churches invite their prospective small-group members to some kind of connection event. These events are intended to help people take small steps toward being in a group, and they are always inspiring and motivational. Here's the usual approach: After a church member has shared a brief testimony on what happened in his life thanks to being in a group last semester, the teaching pastor will say something like, "What a powerful story has just shared. Maybe you know in your heart that you need to be in a group this next semester. If so, I want to invite you to join me and our 40 group leaders this afternoon from 12:30 P.M. to 2:30 P.M. in the gym to learn more about our groups. I hope you will plan to be there, because you will be inspired . . . and we will provide lunch."

Churches that use connection events are well intentioned, but let's think through the logic. Let's say that during Jose's testimony, 50 percent of a 700-person congregation was inspired and open to joining a group. These 350 people are then invited to attend an afternoon group connection lunch the same afternoon or perhaps the following Sunday. How many of the 350 people do you think will show up? Maybe 175; but more realistically, probably only 100 or so. For the other 250, the moment will have passed, they will have other plans, they will have talked themselves out of it or their spouse will have talked them out of it. By adding the connection event step—or any step, for that matter—you will see an exponential decrease in sign-ups as compared to giving people a chance to sign up during the worship service.

Perhaps the logic behind the connection event is that people need a chance to hear more about the commitment they are making to a group. I agree that the commitment needs to be fully explained. But you can explain more after people have signed up. Most people are much more willing to accept the requirements of a group after they've made an initial decision to join; so work with that.

Sure, there will be a few who sign up and then, after learning of the commitments (i.e., after going over the group covenant in the first meeting), decide to postpone being in a group. But this will be a significantly smaller percentage of people than you might expect. People who sign up for a group expect there to be a certain level of commitment. Commitment comes with anything worthwhile that they join. Give your people credit. Church leaders' concern over how people will react to the commitment of joining a group is usually a far greater issue than people's response to group commitment.

Activate Principle

Adding additional steps will exponentially
decrease your total sign-ups.

Some churches make the mistake of asking potential group members to call or email a group leader to get signed up. On the surface, this makes sense. After all, if someone calls or emails a leader to sign up, they can go ahead and get all the group information, make a personal connection and save the church office a little administrative work. But this extra step will keep some people from signing up.

Many people are afraid to call a stranger on the phone, even if they go to the same church. It's quite intimidating for all but the most extroverted personalities. Emailing a group leader is a little better, but again this adds an extra step. Not to mention that, even if a potential member has every intention of emailing a leader and joining, it's easy to put it off, lose the email address, type it in wrong or end up having it get caught in a spam filter. Our job is to make things clear and simple for potential small-group members, not give them excuses.

Asking for too much information throws up another barrier. We've seen some sign-up forms that look more like an IRS publication than a local church discipleship tool. These forms ask for way too much information or are difficult to complete. They are both confusing and complicated and will cause people to say no to joining a group. Here are some guidelines for your sign-up forms:

- *Ask only for basic information*: Name, best phone number and email address. Do you really need their street address? Maybe; but if not, then don't ask for it. The less you want, the more likely they are to comply. Note: When asking for the phone number, simply ask for their "Best Contact Number." This one change dramatically simplified our sign-up form. Most people have multiple phone numbers, but there's only one "best" way to reach them.

- *Make sure the lines or boxes on the forms are big enough for people to write in.* Many sign-up forms are too small, too crowded and too hard to fill out. Provide plenty of space to write. Most people's handwriting is larger than you may anticipate, and it's not uncommon for an email address to be 25 to 30 characters. Have several people around your office fill out the draft before you print hundreds, just to make sure it's user-friendly.

- *Print the sign-up form on cover stock or card stock* so that it will be easy to write on. A slightly thicker form also feels more important.

- *Make your website form just as simple.* Never collect information unless you plan to actually use it. Think simple, quick and clear.

One-step sign-ups are essential. They will mean a little more administrative and follow-up work for you on the back end, but that is okay. The goal is to make things easy for the person joining. The benefits of getting everyone in a group by way of a simple, clear sign-up process far outweighs the work we do to make it happen. This is what we are called to. (For more on what happens after someone signs up for a group, see Fill Factor #10.)

Fill Factor #2: Teaching on the Power of Groups

You've probably heard the expression "When someone's 'why' is strong enough, they'll figure out the 'how'." Well, one of the main reasons people do not join a small group is because they don't have enough reasons "why" to overcome the fact that they may have to step out of their comfort zone. That's why teaching on the power of groups from the stage or pulpit is crucially important. You have to give people a biblical basis for why they need to join a small group. Here are some reasons straight from the Bible:

1. Since the start of the Christian church, Christians have gathered in large groups and in small groups for discipleship, fellowship, worship, evangelism and ministry (see Acts 2:46-47).
2. God created us to be in relationships—with Him and with others (see Gen. 2:18).
3. We need people because life is tough (see Eccles. 4:9-12).
4. Jesus' presence is stronger when two or three are gathered in His name (Matt. 18:20).
5. Fellowship with other believers is part of God's plan for discipleship (Acts 2:41-42).

We could go on and on with the biblical substantiation. The bottom line is that this kind of teaching must be delivered from the stage in a church that is serious about small groups. That's why, as we said earlier, you must generate full staff support if you are going to have the most effective small groups system possible.

Your weekend service and your life groups should have tremendous synergy. In fact, at The Journey, we keep things so simple that if an idea, suggestion or ministry doesn't enhance the weekend service or support life-change through small groups, we don't look at it twice. Our dual focus may be narrow, but we believe that it's the New Testament way. Because of this belief, we make sure that we preach on the need to be in a group at least three times a year, once for each promotion month. Our preaching may surprise you. If you heard the titles of some of the sermons taught in an effort to make people understand the importance of groups, you may not recognize their purpose. Here are some of the titles we've used:

- High-Definition Relationships
- The Power of Positive Relationships
- The High Cost of Following Jesus
- A Place to Call Home
- Finding Community
- Friendships: Wireless Connections
- One: The Loneliest Number
- Why You Need a Group

Okay, maybe that last one was what you might expect! But the point is, you should target how groups will meet people's needs, rather than just hitting the need to be in a group. What is the "why" for those people you are talking to? Go back to the top 10 list you wrote at the beginning of this section. What reasons did you write down? Why should your people be in a group? Think through how the Bible addresses those reasons.

In New York City, loneliness is a big problem. People have a hard time developing relationships with others around them. That's why so many of our groups-promoting messages revolve around themes such as "Find a Home," "Finding a Community," "Overcoming Loneliness," and so forth. How about in your community? If you are a teaching pastor, take a moment and write some potential titles or topics you might address that would resonate with your people:

Topic: _____

Topic: _____

Topic: _____

Title: _____

Title: _____

Title: _____

The key is to find a theme that addresses the felt need (say, loneliness) and then offers God's biblical answer to that need ("consistently putting yourself around people who care about you and your growth . . . And there's no better place to find that than in one of our groups this next semester").

Two words of caution: First, don't *over*estimate the power of the pulpit. Your sermons are only as good as the systems that support them. A powerful sermon on the need to join a small group can be flat-lined if the sign-up card is confusing. Sermons and system work together. Second, don't *under*estimate the power of the pulpit. People want you to preach on the key issues that groups address. It is perfectly appropriate to encourage people to join groups in the context of your sermons.

At The Journey, we rarely make announcements during the service. Small groups and emails emanate the kind of information that announcements usually cover—information that takes people out of the service and comes across as irrelevant to most newcomers. But we do occasionally do what we call "preaching the announcements." That is, if something is highly important to the spiritual development of our congregation, such as baptism or membership or joining a group, we preach on its importance from time to time. Strategically, the best time to preach on small groups is a week or two prior to the beginning of group sign-ups. (For Lead and Teaching Pastor resources on how to plan your preaching to maximize groups, visit www.Activate Books.com.)

Some group leaders may be reading this right now and feel like what was just presented is impossible at your church because the teaching/senior pastor is not 100 percent behind the small-group system. That's a legitimate barrier in some churches. Maybe the senior pastor is not fully sold on groups, or maybe the style of teaching at your church doesn't lend itself to preaching on groups. If this is you, we'd like to encourage you to take these three steps:

1. Continue to support the senior pastor's vision for your church. We hold a high view of this role and encourage you as a staff pastor or leader in the church to ultimately submit to that vision.

2. Commit to doing as many other "Fill Factors" as possible. While teaching on groups is very important, it's possible to run a strong groups system without this key component.

3. Share a copy of this book with your senior pastor and arrange a follow-up meeting to discuss it.

Your pastor is God's leader of your church, and I strongly encourage you to fully support him or her even if it means you have to ignore some of the advice we are sharing in this book.

At the same time, some senior/teaching pastor may be reading this right now and you are very motivated to start teaching on the power of groups. We hope so! But let me caution you just a bit too. First, remember that your sermon on groups is part of the overall groups system. Be sure to support the full system and don't get so caught up with your sermon that other details you should attend to fall through the cracks. Second, in your sermons, be sure not to oversell groups. Groups are a very important part of any church's life and ministry, but take care that you don't go too far by using such phrases as:

- "If you aren't in a group at our church, then you're only getting half of what God has to offer you here."
- "If you say no to being in a group, then you are saying no to God's best for your life."
- "You are sinning if you are not in a group."

These are actual statements we've heard pastors make! And we aren't completely innocent ourselves. Early on, when we were developing this groups system, someone accused our teaching team of preaching so hard about the need for groups that it sounded as if not being in a group would condemn you to hell. That may have been overselling a bit!

While we want as many people as possible to experience life-change in a strong groups system, we fully recognize that a person can grow spiritually and get a lot out of participating in a church even if he or she chooses not to join a group. Also, there are times when someone really wants to be in a group but circumstances make it impossible—a single mother with a new baby, someone with a new job that requires a lot of travel, or someone going back to school at night, to name a few. As much as we hate to admit it, sometimes being in a group just isn't feasible, for the time being anyway. Allow people to take a break from being in a group when there are exceptional circumstances; just don't let them be out of a group too long without checking in with them.

Teaching pastors, don't let promotion months be the only time of year that you mention groups from the pulpit. Groups should be a common thread that shows up regularly in your sermons. You can create a culture of groups in your church by talking about groups, highlighting groups and raising the value of groups in sermons throughout the year. Here are some ideas on how to pepper your sermons to support group life:

1. Talk about your group. You are in a group, right?

2. Share stories about what particular groups are doing.

3. Talk about someone you met when visiting a group recently.

4. If you are introducing a testimony of any kind, tell people what group the person giving the testimony is in or was recently in.

5. When teaching a text that has a natural tie-in to groups, make a point to say, "This is why we value small groups at

our church." You don't have to challenge people to sign up right then and there, but you can raise the value with your comments.

6. Compliment people for being in a group, or compliment group leaders.

7. Remind people to stay strong in their groups. This is especially important during the middle of a semester.

8. Encourage people to get back in a group or switch groups if they feel out of place. This ties in well with themes like endurance, flexibility or getting outside of your comfort zone.

If your groups pastor is a gifted speaker, let him or her teach from time to time so that people see that you value this important role. One caution: Don't have the groups pastor teach only during promotion months. In fact, we would say it's better for the main teacher to teach during the promotion months to mobilize the most people for groups. At The Journey, we've had the groups pastor co-teach during promotion months, but we want the main voice of our church to be the one calling people to commitment.

When you teach on groups, you help the groups culture become fully integrated into the life of your church. Preach on groups just like you would preach on reading the Bible, praying, giving, serving or any other action of discipleship. There is power in presenting the biblical basis for groups and challenging people to step up.

Fill Factor #3: Testimonies, Videos and Dramas

Human experience speaks volumes. When we see human experience portrayed, and that we can relate to, we are often spurred to action. That's why testimonies, videos and dramas are such a powerful tool to encourage group sign-ups. They can be used to supplement a sermon on small groups, or they can stand alone.

Testimonies are particularly effective. When you have a small groups testimony from someone that is personal, passionate and persuasive, people will connect with what is being said. During your promotion months, make it a goal to have one or two testimonies on the power of groups. You can either work these testimonies in as part of the sermon or use them at a different point in the worship experience that Sunday.

Activate Principle

Next to preaching on the biblical basis for groups, testimonies are the most powerful way to motivate people to join.

As we write this, we are two weeks away from the start of our next groups semester. We are excited to have a wonderful couple in our church scheduled to give a testimony. They'll talk about how being in a group has strengthened their relationship with God and with each other. They'll also tell everyone how being in a group led to meeting and developing friendships with other couples in our church. We know what they are going to say because anyone who shares a testimony from the stage of The Journey is required to submit their notes a few days in advance. This allows us to give some feedback, and it helps us prepare the best way to introduce them. In this case, the husband and wife will be on stage together. Their presence and testimony will be powerful. Since they are both group leaders, we're certain their group will fill up right after they finish the first service and, since they are a couple, their testimony will benefit all of the couples' groups scheduled for the coming semester. They are a real-life demonstration to everyone in the crowd that what we say about groups is true.

This testimony will be live. The couple will speak in all of our services. But sometimes it's better to do a video testimony, especially if the testimony is very emotional and it would be difficult to share it at multiple services. Video testimonies have a lot of benefits: You can tape them well in advance, you know exactly what is going to be said and you know how long it will take. Once, we had a guy in our church share about how he almost committed suicide, but it was the support of his group that kept him from following through. We filmed him talking for more than 20 minutes and then edited the video to the most powerful 6 minutes. This would have been an impossible testimony to give live in every service. We still hear people talking about the impact that testimony had on them.

Not all of our testimonies are so dramatic. Most of the time, we ask someone to share who has had a "normal" group experience. They talk about the discipline of going to group each week, the struggle to do the lessons, the fun or friendships they have experienced and how they grew closer to God. The testifiers don't have to be well-trained public speakers. Even if someone is clearly reading from notes, the story can still have a tremendous impact on the congregation. The more "normal" the people giving a testimony are, the more relatable they will be to the masses. You have stories in your church too. Find people who have experienced the power of groups and ask them to share their story from the stage or pulpit.

In addition to testimonies, you can also use videos to promote and enhance group sign-ups. Sometimes these are video testimonies like the ones we mentioned, but most of the time they are videos that describe groups, highlight types of groups or make people laugh about their fear of joining a group. We once did an entire series of videos that were designed to poke fun at people's apprehension about joining a group. Sometimes these are custom videos using people or groups in our church; other times they are cleverly edited clips from movies; and sometimes they are resources we purchase or borrow from other churches. The key is to use a two- to three-minute punchy video that supports groups, draws people in and encourages sign-ups.

Finally, never underestimate the power of drama. We could be accused of erring on the humorous side when it comes to dramas, but we love to make people laugh at the silly excuses they give for not being in a group. Dramas are less effective than testimonies and often more difficult to prepare than video, but they can be powerful, especially if people in the church can truly relate to what the actors are experiencing.

We've done it all—from monologues to multi-part series—and different ones have different effects. There's an element of trial and error when dealing in the arts. Just keep pushing your creativity level and God may work in ways and through forms of persuasion you would never have imagined.

Fill Factor #4: Small Groups Info Table

As mentioned earlier in the Fill section, the Groups Information Table is one way for prospective joiners to sign up for a group. Located in your lobby, the table gives those interested in signing up a place to meet group leaders, see the curricula being studied and have their questions answered. When you first start your small groups system, you'll probably be able to put all of your leaders at the table each week. But as your church grows and your number of groups increases, you'll need to rotate leaders. At The Journey, we have our group leaders sign up to work the table either before or after the service a couple of times during the promotion month. Often, we'll try to use the leaders of groups that haven't filled up yet so that they can recruit for their own groups.

Before you put your group leaders behind the table, quickly brief them on how to answer the common questions they'll be asked:

- Why should I join a group, or why should I join *your* group?
- How long are the groups in session?

- Is there a group for my unique needs (married, single, kids)?
- How do I sign up?
- What if I join a group but don't like it?
- Where do I buy the book/curriculum?

Encourage your group leaders to give a compassionate answer, no matter how basic the question, and give each person a sign-up card and invite them to join on the spot.

Because we are a portable church that rents our space on Sundays, our groups tables are clearly recognized but are not overly designed. We often put an element of fun at the table, such as balloons or candy. Be creative and make your table as attractive as possible. You don't have to be extravagant or have a table that could win a trade show exhibit award. Just set up a simple place where people can ask questions and meet leaders. Many people who do not actually walk up to the table will walk by and be motivated to join a group just by seeing the commitment of the leaders behind the tables each week.

The groups table has a great side benefit for your leaders. After serving behind the table, group leaders tend to walk away with an increased sense of responsibility to fill their groups. As we've said earlier, making sure that each leader takes responsibility to fill his or her group beyond what is done as a church is key to a successful groups semester. Sometimes a great leader can have a group that is slow to fill up for any number of reasons. Maybe the group meets the same night as a lot of other groups, or the time is not convenient, or the study is not popular. Your job is to keep these leaders motivated and give them opportunities to fill their groups—opportunities like the groups table.

Fill Factor #5: Targeting Specific Groups Types

Once you have the first four Fill Factors in place, start thinking about narrowing your focus to more of a select audience. You can catch a lot of sign-ups by targeting specific types of people with specific types of groups. Target people based on their life stage, interests or occupation. For example, invite couples to join a couples' group. Invite business people to join a professionals' group. The key to maximizing this Fill Factor will lie in your database. Think about it: You'll have a hard time targeting married couples if you don't know who the married couples in your church are.

Activate Principle
Good data will help you get good sign-up results.

We've mentioned that we have a large number of artists at The Journey. They are a unique sub-segment of our congregation. You probably have large sub-segments as well—perhaps retirees, single parents, college-age kids, and so forth. The first time we offered an artists' group, it was literally one group that met over lunch. Interestingly, after we had been offering artists' groups for a couple of semesters, a few artists came to us with a concern. They let us know that we didn't need to offer artists' groups anymore, because the artists in the church didn't want to be singled out. They wanted to integrate with the rest of the church.

The next semester we did not offer any artists' groups. Nor did we offer any the semester after that. Then, after two semesters without artists' groups, we looked at some data. We pulled the list of artists in groups from the previous year and compared that to the current number of artists in groups. The current number was significantly lower. Even one of the artists who had approached us had dropped out of groups completely. We called him, and he said, "You know, the people in my last group just didn't get me. I'm an artist and my world is so different from theirs." Of course. We started offering artists' groups again, and that sub-segment of our church has flourished in groups ever since. Now, at least 10 percent of our groups are geared toward artists.

So, why do we offer groups that are just for artists? Because artists have a different set of needs, they operate on a different schedule and, in general, they think in slightly different ways. Since artists lead these groups, we let them choose the time, location and curriculum. In our promotion, we simply list that the group is for artists. We don't define what that means. We let those who sign up determine whether or not they fall into this broad category. To be clear, these artist-focused groups are just like all of our other groups, in every way. They start and end the semester at the same time, the members pray together, they meet for 90 minutes, and so forth. The only real difference we have observed is that our artists' groups rarely meet early in the morning!

Obviously, artists are not forced to join an artists' group. Some artists would rather be in a group with non-artists, just as I've heard some retirees say they want to be in a group with non-retirees. Let each person choose what kind of group he or she wants to join. But know that by creating targeted groups you will increase your sign-up rate and better meet the needs of a significant number of people. Simply identify the large sub-segments in your church with particular needs and offer groups designed just for them. As you do, you will want to target communication or promotion to them in order to fill the group.

You can target these sub-segments as part of your promotion month. About three weeks before the semester begins, we start targeting. For example, our worship arts pastor, who ultimately oversees all of our artists' groups, starts contacting every artist he knows of in the church—by phone, email or text message—to make sure they are in a group. As he does this, other sub-segments are also being contacted. For example, another coach might be contacting singles while another contacts college students. We'll also be highlighting certain types of groups from the stage on Sundays. We might bring all the artists' groups leaders on stage at one time and introduce them, for instance. On this day we would also have targeted group leaders serving before and after the services at the groups table.

Let's look to community service groups for one more example. One time, we had a group that was basically a general group, but the members were going to do a community service project during the semester to help the homeless in our city. How do you fill this group? There's no database checkbox in our software that tells us if someone has compassion for the homeless. Well, about a month before this group was promoted, we had a "coat drive" in the weekend service. We hadn't announced it in advance; we just picked what was certain to be a cold day, taught a message on compassion for those in need and then literally asked people to give the coats off their backs. What a powerful day!

During that service, we collected the names of everyone who had given a coat—several hundred people. We invited people from that coat drive list to be a part of this community service group. As you can imagine, the group filled up with very passionate and compassionate people. In fact, instead of doing one project to help the homeless, they did a project after their group study almost every week. This testimony has been a catalyst for our community service groups every semester since.

Take just a moment to list the types of groups your church is currently offering. Brainstorm some ways that you could reach out to people who may be interested in those groups but are not yet connected.

GROUP TYPE   **PROMOTION IDEA**

_____   _____

_____   _____

_____   _____

_____   _____

_____   _____

_____   _____

_____   _____

Fill Factor #6: The Church-wide Campaign

Every fall semester at The Journey, we do a church-wide campaign, or integrated movement, where small-group discussions mirror and support sermon topics, and vice versa. Recently, we did a church-wide campaign called "The New Testament Challenge." The start date for the Sunday teaching series was the same week as the start date for the groups semester. We challenged our people to read through the New Testament in 63 days to coincide with the Sunday teachings, which were oriented around the key themes of the New Testament, and to discuss the readings in their groups throughout the week. The challenge was very effective for group sign-ups, and really had an impact on our church by deepening each group member's walk with God. Tremendous synergy occurs in a church when there is a single focus between the Sunday service and small groups.

Sometimes people see groups as an add-on. They think groups are just part of the buffet the church offers—another option for spiritual growth besides the weekend service. A united campaign helps people see that groups do not stand alone. Rather, they are an integral part of the whole life of the church. When they understand this unity, people who have never experienced the power of groups are more likely to sign up. That means that first-time group members are more likely to sign up during the church-wide campaign semester than during any other semester.

We recommend using a church-wide campaign one semester a year. Fall and spring are the two best options, with fall winning by a nose. In our experience, with hundreds of churches, fall semester church-wide campaigns seem to generate the most sign-ups. Why? Because of the back-to-school urge that lies dormant (or not so dormant) in each of us. The fall feels like the beginning of a new semester, even to people who have never been in a small group before. That's what you want. Work with the inherent tendencies of the fall season. Fall also lends itself to a church-wide campaign because the Thanksgiving holiday makes the semester a little shorter. This means that you will have an easier time coordinating small groups with the Sunday service. Here's what a typical fall campaign might look like:

Campaign: The New Testament Challenge

September:
Promotion Month

October 1 (Monday):
First week of groups. This is the introduction meeting, where people get to know each other, go over the groups covenant and receive the syllabus.

October 7 (Sunday):
The New Testament Challenge begins.

October 8 (Monday):
This week, groups discuss curriculum for the first time.

October 14–November 17:
The New Testament Challenge continues with Sunday sermons and weekly group studies.

November 18 (Sunday):
New Testament Challenge sermon #7

November 19 (Monday):
No group meetings due to Thanksgiving holiday

November 25 (Sunday):
New Testament Challenge sermon #8

December 2 (Sunday):
Final New Testament Challenge worship Service/celebration Sunday

December 15 (Saturday):
All New Testament Challenge groups conclude by this date.

If you look at this calendar carefully, you will notice that there are 9 New Testament Challenge sermons and 11 group meetings. These additional meetings are no problem. So what do you do with them? We encourage all of our groups to have a "play date" during one of their scheduled meetings. Instead of having small group, they do something else together—go out to dinner, go bowling, etc. The other extra week can be a wrap-up week, when the group meets to discuss key lessons they've learned throughout the semester and have a final party.

As important as the calendar is, a little wiggle room is usually needed during the church-wide campaign. Nine weeks is a long time for a sermon series, and to stretch it to 11 weeks may be impossible. But you can easily end the Sunday part of the campaign before your groups completely wrap up. There have been times when we have run the calendar as shown but ended the Sunday sermon series the Sunday before Thanksgiving. Groups still meet through the middle of December. In this case, we provide a two- to three-week mini-study on a key topic, such as "How to Share Your Faith at Christmas." So even if your sermon series ends before the campaign, you can still keep groups together and finish the semester strong.

Doing a church-wide campaign requires an extra level of planning above and beyond a normal groups semester. It requires a higher than normal level of communication between the teaching and worship teams and the small groups team. However, there is one area where you get a big break during the church-wide campaign: the groups catalog. Because all of the groups are studying the same curriculum, the catalog is easier to design and prepare. Accept that breather with thanks as you throw yourself into the rest of the planning. Church-wide campaigns are more than worth the work you invest. The united focus they bring leads to hearts open to spiritual growth and true life-change.

A word of caution: Because the church-wide campaign does take a lot of energy to get off the ground, reserve some time and vigor to plan for the semester after the church-wide campaign. Some churches have had great campaigns only to see their small groups system crash the next semester because of negligent planning. Continuing with our Four Fs model, as soon as your groups are off and running (Facilitate), make sure you move back to Focus and Form so that the following semester you are ready with even more life-changing groups.

A church-wide campaign is the best way to initiate a brand-new semester-based groups system. Yes, doing a campaign is more difficult than doing a regular semester of groups. But because it involves the whole church and the majority of the staff, it's a great way to either launch small groups in your church or to shift to the semester-based groups system in this book. If at all possible, we highly recommend that you start your groups system with a church-wide campaign. Not only will it help you fill your groups, but it will also set you on the right path for future success.

Fill Factor #7: Newsletters and Mailings

You simply cannot overcommunicate the need to join a group during the promotion month. People need to hear the same thing over and over again before they actually *hear* it. As all good marketing professionals know, repetition works. And when you can vary the form of that repetition, all the better!

Activate Principle
Promotion months require creative redundancy—
saying the same thing but in new and different ways.

From your perspective, you may feel like you've been talking so much about groups that *surely* everyone has heard. Not necessarily. We've learned that about the time we're getting tired of talking up the need to be in a group, people in our congregation are just starting to get the message. So we have to keep saying it over and over again in creative ways for those who are there most weeks and for those who aren't. Some of the people who consider your church their home may not have been in a service since you started promotions. How are you going to reach them? This is where the newsletter and mailings come in.

The church newsletter is a ubiquitous tool. Let's look at how we can use this tool to Fill groups in either of its two common forms.

The Printed Newsletter

Even though a printed newsletter might seem a little old school these days, it has some advantages over the e-newsletter alternative. First of all, it will be delivered where you send it, since there are no spam blockers at the local post office. Second, it has some staying power. An actual newsletter may hang around someone's home for a week or so and not be immediately banished by the person on receipt. Third, multiple people in one household read the same printed material. Finally, you can often tell a longer story in a printed newsletter than in an e-newsletter.

In your printed newsletter, be creative in promoting groups. Go beyond the standard words "you need to be in a group" and push and surprise people with something fresh. Here are a few thoughts:

- Capture people's hearts by teaching them something about the biblical basis of groups. Include a Bible study they can do on their own.
- Share small-group testimonies from peers in the church.
- Promote specific types of groups in greater detail.
- Teach the uninitiated how to sign up for a group online.

- Lay out the groups calendar.
- Highlight certain group leaders.
- Use the newsletter in any other way to Fill groups.

Even if you don't have a printed newsletter at your church anymore, you could do a special mailing during your promotion months. Some churches simply mail a postcard intended to drive people to their website to sign up. Others get quite elaborate and send out a magazine-style mailing that is part inspiration and part catalog. Be as creative as you want to be in your printed mailings. Just make sure you clearly show people why they should join a group and how to join when they are ready. And don't forget to track whether or not your mailings are working so that you can continue to improve from one semester to the next.

The E-Newsletter

Most churches now use some form of e-newsletter to communicate to the congregation. E-newsletters have several advantages over printed newsletters, especially when it comes to filling your groups. First of all, they cost almost nothing to send. Second, you can include a direct link to your groups sign-up page. Third, they can be easily forwarded to friends and colleagues who may be interested in groups. Finally, they require less advanced planning than a traditional newsletter. We recommend that you start using your e-newsletter to promote sign-ups as soon as your promotion month begins. As the semester's start date gets closer, increase the space dedicated to groups. Make the ads, the articles and the testimonies for groups more prominent. A week or two prior to the start of groups, you might do an entire newsletter focused on groups.

While the key to an effective printed newsletter is the ability to touch the heart, the key to an e-newsletter is carefully worded, good copy that moves people to action. If the following sentences were hyperlinks to our groups online sign-up page, which one would you click on?

- Group sign-ups have begun. Click here!
- Have you taken the New Testament Challenge? Learn more here!

Both are strong. Combine one of these headlines with a catchy email subject line and some motivating explanatory text and you have a nice e-newsletter promotion. There are dozens of books on writing effective e-newsletter copy that you may want to check out. But for now, think clarity, simplicity and wording that spur them to action.

If your church does not currently do an e-newsletter, you might give it a test run during your next Fill month. If you are already using an e-newsletter, you might try adding electronic communication tools available via text messaging or Web 2.0 applications. Remember, the printed newsletter or the e-newsletter is a complement to what you do on the weekend and online. Make sure your most effective Fill Factors are fully functioning before you invest time in this one.

Fill Factor #8: Selling the Previously Sold

An old business adage says, "Your best customer is the one you've already got!" The same principle applies to small groups. Reaching out specifically to those who have been in a group before will help you fill your new groups.

To utilize this Fill Factor effectively, keep a clean database with the names and contact information of everyone who signs up for a group each semester. A week or two into your promotion month, pull the database from the previous semester and compare it with your sign-ups. See who is not yet in a new group. Good database technology makes this much easier than it sounds. We did it for years using a simple compare script in Excel. Reach out to everyone who has not signed up for the coming semester. Here is an email we sent during the Fill month for our New Testament Challenge:

Activate

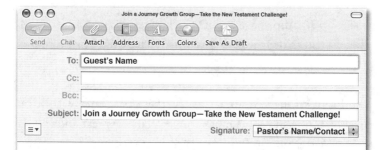

Don't miss your chance to be a part of a New Testament Challenge Growth Group at The Journey this Fall! The Journey's Fall Growth Groups begin the first week in October and last through mid-December. So, today is a great time to sign up!

Growth Groups are The Journey's groups of 12-15 people that get together weekly in convenient locations all over the metro New York area to meet new friends, have fun and grow spiritually.

All of our Fall Growth Groups will be reading through the New Testament together in just 63 days. Have you ever read the entire New Testament? Most people haven't, and even if you have, imagine the spiritual impact in your life of reading it again with the entire church. Don't let this chance to take the New Testament Challenge pass you by. It's easy to sign up.

1. Visit The Journey's Growth Groups online at www.journeymetro.com/gg.
2. Sign up for the Growth Group you are most interested in.
3. Have a blast attending your Growth Group this Fall!

(You can also sign up for a Growth Group at any Journey Sunday service.) There are close to 80 different groups to choose from! So, sign up today at http://www.journeymetro.com/gg

Let me know if you have any questions or if I can serve you in any way. I hope you decide to get connected in a New Testament Challenge Growth Group this Fall.

See you on Sunday!
Pastor Kerrick

P.S.—Join us this Sunday as we continue our teaching series "Fully Engaged: The Power of a Committed Life."

Kerrick Thomas
Executive Pastor, The Journey Church
www.journeymetro.com

This simple email was all the encouragement that many of our former group members needed to sign up. A little push like this is especially effective for those who have been in groups consistently. They sometimes need a reminder that they have to sign up every semester.

Activate Principle

The best potential group members for the upcoming semester are people who were in groups the previous semester.

You could also craft this email a little differently and use it to reach those who took the previous semester off, or maybe those who have been inactive for a couple of semesters. You may need to address their specific concerns. We've sent letters and emails that begin, "Maybe it has been a while since you've been in a group because you had a bad experience with your last group. As much as we hate to admit it, this happens from time to time. I'm sorry if it happened to you, but I hope you won't let one imperfect experience keep you from experiencing the spiritual growth opportunity you have this coming semester . . ." We might conclude this note by offering to personally discuss any of their concerns or to help them find a good group fit. Just by acknowledging their feelings, you will take a big step toward getting them back in groups.

One caution: Don't waste a lot of time or energy going after people who have serious issues with your church, or who have given up on groups. If someone has left your church, don't try to pull him or her back in with groups. Do not reach out to church hoppers or to that small number of people who are dissatisfied with virtually everything the church does. Better that they don't join a group! There's only one exception: If an unbeliever was attending your church but has pulled away, you can use the upcoming groups semester as a way to get them back on track toward God.

Fill Factor #9: Promoting Groups to Newcomers

Not only do newcomers make great group members, but their involvement is also critical for both them and you! You will be doing well to fill your groups with as many of your new attenders as possible. As I (Nelson) suggested in *Fusion: Turning First Time Guests into Fully Engaged Members of Your Church*, start educating and promoting groups to newcomers soon after their first visit. If God has sent a first- or second-time guest to your church, He is working in his or her life and has invited you to be a part of what He wants to do in this person. We believe that you have a sacred responsibility to assimilate the person into your church; connecting him or her in your small groups system goes a long way toward accomplishing that goal.

Newcomers are good for groups, and groups are good for newcomers. Your new people will have a fresh excitement that is contagious. And because they don't have to be Christians to be in a group, a groups semester gives them the perfect opportunity to belong before they believe. They'll be able to start developing relationships with some godly people, allowing them to get an up-close and personal look at what it means to live for Christ.

We have had people who were not yet Christians join a group and, with that group, start studying the Bible, start praying and even start doing servant evangelism. It's usually not long at all before they decide to turn their lives over to Jesus Christ. When they do, the entire group can celebrate with them and support them. So getting newcomers into groups is a critical step for their spiritual development and one that can help you fill your groups with new, excited faces.

The process for correctly inviting newcomers to join a group is simple but requires the following effort and planning:

1. Pull a list of all your first- and second-time guests from the previous four months.

2. Pray over this list. Thank God that He has entrusted you with these newcomers.

3. Prepare a targeted mailing or email, inviting everyone on this list to join a group this semester. You may even want to highlight a few groups that would be perfect for those new to the church.

You can also promote groups to your newcomers during non-promotion months. Just take the first opportunity you have to explain the importance of groups and let them know when next semester's sign-ups begin. At The Journey, we give them a brochure about groups and a link to the groups information on our website. We also invite newcomers to "play groups," where they can meet people from other groups while a semester is in full swing. (For more on play groups, visit www.ActivateBook.com.) Newcomers never mind waiting until the next semester to sign up. In fact, their anticipation works in everyone's favor. Here's an example of a letter that second-time guests receive within 96 hours of their visit to our church. Notice how groups are mentioned.

Hi [guest's name],

It was great seeing you again at The Journey on Sunday! We hope you had a fun and meaningful experience with us as we talked about "Friendship: Wireless Connections."

We're excited that you chose to check out The Journey a second time, and we want to do something nice for you to show our appreciation. Enclosed is a $5 gift card to Starbucks. Take a friend and have a good time!

This month is a great time to sign up for a Growth Group at The Journey. Growth Groups are The Journey's small groups of 8 to 12 people who meet together weekly. You can sign up for the group of your choice on Sunday or online at www.journeymetro.com.

Please let us know if there is anything we can do for you or if there is a specific way that we can be praying for you this week. Also, let us know if you have any questions about The Journey and how you can get plugged in further.

To find out more about The Journey and all that's going on, be sure to visit our website at www.journeymetro.com.

We look forward to seeing you on Sunday. Have a great week, and God bless! On the journey together,

Nelson

Nelson Searcy, Lead Pastor
The Journey
www.journeymetro.com

P.S. Don't forget—This weekend we continue Life360 by examining how we can have a high-definition faith. You will not want to miss it! Invite a friend to come with you. We look forward to seeing you then.

For more on how group promotion complements and supports assimilation, see *Fusion: Turning First Time Guests into Fully Engaged Members of Your Church* by Nelson Searcy and Jennifer Dykes Henson.

Activate Principle
Every newcomer God entrusts to your church should receive a clear, heartfelt invitation to be in a group the coming semester.

Fill Factor #10: Creating Urgency

Creating urgency around the sign-up process will help you fill your groups. People respond to a sense of urgency. As a species, we do not do what we ought to do when we ought to do it, but we do what we have to do when we have to do it!

There are three ways to use the natural calendar flow of the groups system to create urgency that people will respond to.

1. *Set a clear deadline for sign-ups.* In reality, someone can join a group several weeks after kick-off, but they don't need to know that up front. You should be creating a sense of urgency by constantly reminding people to "sign up for a group today because groups begin in two weeks." Some people will wait until the very last minute, so spur them to action by keeping the start date clearly in front of them. We heard about one church that actually used a countdown clock for the number of days left to sign up for a group. On the last sign-up Sunday, the countdown switched from days to hours, then minutes, then seconds left to join!

2. *Each week, announce how many groups have filled up.* As people see that their choices are getting slimmer the longer they wait to join, they are more likely to go ahead and take the step. After doing this for a few semesters, you will start seeing some who are natural procrastinators actually rush to sign up so that they can get into their first choice group.

3. *Tell people how many sign-ups there are.* At first glance, this seems to be a tool that promotes the success of the groups system rather than creating urgency around sign-ups; but remember what we said earlier: People want to be on the bandwagon. They want to do what everyone else is doing and they want to be a part of something successful. When you first introduce this groups system in your church, there may be a few who will hold out because they don't

believe it's going to succeed. By underscoring the success, you will motivate those hiding in the bushes to action.

Activate Principle

People do not do what's important; they do what is urgent.

Urgency motivates people to action. Work with this truth, create excitement and fill those groups!

Fill Factor #11: No Sign-Up Left Behind

Here is your final Fill Factor: Make sure that no one who signs up is left behind. Everyone who signs up at the worship service or online must be placed on a list for follow-up. It's all too easy for sign-up cards to get lost, data to go un-entered or phone calls/emails to go unanswered. Don't let this happen to you! We jokingly tell churches to treat group sign-ups with the same care as the offering (double counters, security bags, immediate attention on Monday morning, etc.). Maybe that's not such a bad practice after all! The people who sign up for groups are a precious commodity.

How We Handle Sign-Ups at The Journey

When a person signs up for a group on a Sunday—either on the back of their Connection Card or at the groups table—his or her information gets entered into our system that afternoon or Monday morning. By Monday afternoon at the latest, we have a list of everyone who signed up and what group they signed up for. Then, we do two things.

1. We email everyone who signed up for a group, thank them and let them know they will be hearing from their group leader shortly with all of the group's pertinent information. Below is a draft of an email we have used in the past:

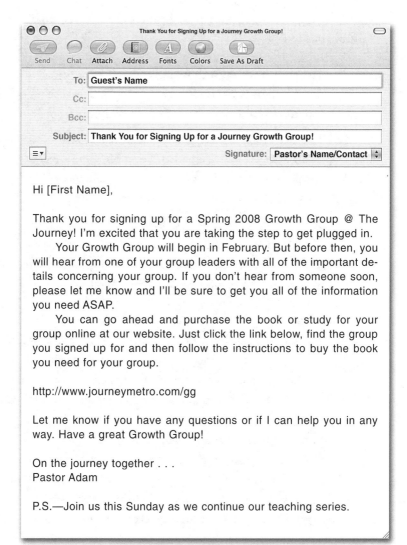

Hi [First Name],

Thank you for signing up for a Spring 2008 Growth Group @ The Journey! I'm excited that you are taking the step to get plugged in.

Your Growth Group will begin in February. But before then, you will hear from one of your group leaders with all of the important details concerning your group. If you don't hear from someone soon, please let me know and I'll be sure to get you all of the information you need ASAP.

You can go ahead and purchase the book or study for your group online at our website. Just click the link below, find the group you signed up for and then follow the instructions to buy the book you need for your group.

http://www.journeymetro.com/gg

Let me know if you have any questions or if I can help you in any way. Have a great Growth Group!

On the journey together . . .
Pastor Adam

P.S.—Join us this Sunday as we continue our teaching series.

2. We forward the name, email and best contact phone number of every sign-up to the leader of the group they signed up for. We encourage groups leaders to follow up with all of their sign-ups as soon as possible.

When a person signs up for a group online, three emails are automatically sent:

1. The person who just signed up receives an automated thank-you response for joining a group and lets the person know that his or her leader will be in touch soon.

2. The leader(s) of that group receives an automated email with the name, email and best phone number of the person who just signed up. This email encourages the leader to contact the new sign-up as soon as possible with all pertinent group information.

3. The Journey staff receives an automated email letting us know who just signed up and for what group so that we can record the information in our database.

All online sign-up systems operate a little differently. You may or may not have the capability of using automated emails. As long as all three of these things happen—the joiner gets confirmed, the leader gets the information and the staff gets notified—you will be in good shape. The key is to make sure that no one slips through the cracks in the follow-up process.

God has entrusted you and your church with each and every person who signs up for a group. Don't take that responsibility lightly. Treat every person who signs up with care. Follow up with each one in a way that will give him or her the best possible reason and opportunity to follow through on this big decision and show up for the group.

Facilitating Your Groups

Facilitate

Careful planning puts you ahead in the long run;
hurry and scurry puts you further behind.

PROVERBS 21:5, *THE MESSAGE*

Everything to this point has been preparation. You have prepared your groups philosophy, recruited group leaders and promoted and filled your groups. Now the group experience begins. Just as when you prepare a fine dinner, the quality of the meal is determined well before your guest sits down to eat. Yet until the guest actually partakes of the food, there is no satisfaction, enjoyment or benefit. All the preparation you have done for your small groups was strategically designed to help ensure the desired result. But none of it pays off until the groups begin and life-change happens. Facilitation is the final step.

Depending on your calendar, February, June and October will most likely be your Facilitation months. Although these months are critically important, in many ways they are the easiest months of your small groups year. But that doesn't mean that Facilitation should be taken lightly. If you have done Focus, Form and Fill well, you are like a football team on the two-yard line. You are about to score a touchdown, but there are two yards to go that cannot be underestimated. You can't let down your guard and think that success is guaranteed. Take a deep breath, motivate your team in the huddle and then go the distance.

Note that while Facilitation is assigned to three specific months, it will actually be expressed throughout the semester. As we will see, there are certain activities to complete just before the assigned Facilitation months (like leaders' training), other activities to complete during the Facilitation months and still others that are done throughout the entire semester (such as week-to-week communication between the groups pastor and the leaders). Successful Facilitation starts before the first group meeting and continues until the semester officially ends.

In this section, we will examine several key Facilitation steps.

1. How to train your group leaders to lead
2. How to manage groups
3. How to maintain quality control with the groups
4. How to create an environment for life-change to occur
5. How to mobilize groups for evangelism
6. How to ensure that groups are an integral part of the life of your church

Facilitate Principle #1: Training Group Leaders

As we said in Big Idea #10, we expect leaders to be facilitators, not experts. We expect them to be great managers of the group environment so that maximum life-change can occur. Therefore, our job is to train them primarily in the nuts and bolts of operating a successful group. This does not mean that we ignore theological training, but it does mean that we expect a group leader to run a strong group even if he or she cannot answer every question raised. It's possible to provide a great group experience, where intense life-change happens, even when a group leader may have to say, "I don't know" every once in a while. In fact, we've discovered that this may be one of the keys to an open, honest and interactive group experience.

So how do we train leaders to facilitate? With a half-day Group Leaders' Training event before the start of each semester and through timely electronic training every week.

Group Leaders Training

About three weeks before the start of every semester, we hold a half-day training session for all group leaders. The exact date is not important. You can choose anything that works well with your calendar; just make sure that it is neither too close to or too far from the beginning of the semester. Because of the timing, this training actually falls in the Fill month. But since it is so crucial to Facilitation, we wanted to save it for this section.

Maybe right now you're asking one of the following questions: "Did you really mean only one half-day training per semester?" "Shouldn't you train leaders before listing them in the catalog?" "That's close to the start of the semester. Shouldn't it be earlier?" "Do returning leaders have to attend even if they did a great job last semester?"

Allow us to address your concerns.

"Did You Really Mean Only One Half-day Training per Semester?"
Yes, we mean only one training event per semester—half of a day, max. We've found that a shorter training session can actually be significantly more effective than a longer session. It forces you to keep a tight agenda and focus on only the core competencies or practices that need to be taught. Any kind of meeting will expand to fit the time you allot for it. We decided that a directed, strong, three-hour meeting would train our people better than stretching the material into a six-hour training. We cover everything we need to cover while we have our leaders' full attention spans.

Activate Principle

Since facilitation is the key to leading a group effectively, the training can be done in a shorter period of time.

Focus your training on the few ideas that really matter, and maximize the time that your leaders have invested. When you respect your people and their time, they have a higher level of respect for what you are asking of them. We have noticed that a shorter meeting also increases the percentage of leaders who attend. Since we aren't asking for an entire weekend or even an entire day, the barriers to attending (such as clearing a schedule, finding a baby-sitter) are a lot easier to break through.

If you do three half-day training events per year—one before each semester—that is a total of nine training hours. Not bad. And if people are better able to absorb all nine hours because the training is delivered in bite-size chunks, then you have made a significant investment in your leaders. In addition, because the training is ongoing every few months, you have an opportunity to frequently reinforce key areas so that they really stick in your leaders' minds. And don't forget or underestimate the apprentice element that is built into the small groups system. The most valuable leadership training any group leader receives comes from serving with a veteran leader in a previous group. We have found that one semester of "on the job" training in a group provides more valuable preparation than all of the outside training you could possibly pull together in a year.

"Shouldn't You Train Leaders Before Listing Them in the Catalog?"
There is a difference between training leaders and selecting leaders. Leaders are selected and approved through the apprentice system. Either they have served with a current group leader, have been recommended by someone in a leadership position, or both. This happens well before the Group Leaders Training. Your approval of a potential leader is based on previous group participation, recommendation and at the person's agreement to be trained at a later time.

Selecting first and training later allows us to raise new leaders more effectively. Not to mention, it places the weight of potential leader recommendations and decisions on those at the most informed levels. After all, the leader who has served with a potential leader can best gauge that person's capacity to lead. Just because a potential leader has completed a more rigorous training program—a requirement in many churches—does not necessarily mean that the person is going to be effective in the group environment.

Training cannot select leaders; it can only equip leaders. Allow the apprentice model to select your leaders, and once they are selected, train them well.

"That's Close to the Start of the Semester. Shouldn't It Be Earlier?"
When the training event is close to the start of the semester, leaders are more inclined to want to learn how to lead. It's a fact of human nature. We don't usually learn what we need to learn until we have to. And a hungry audience makes for an exciting training environment. The proximity to reality also leads to better retention. If facilitation training is too far way from when the actual facilitation will be done, people are more likely to forget what they have been taught.

Activate Principle
People do not go to training when they should go;
they go when they need to go.

When you schedule the training as close to the start date as possible, you can utilize the training to support other areas of your groups system. For example, if the training is held two weeks out, a leader will already know whether or not their group is full. If it isn't, you can use part of the training to motivate them to fill their group. At the same time, you may have to use the training to combine groups if several are at risk, or to adjust topics, times and locations to increase sign-ups.

"Do Returning Leaders Have to Attend Even if They Did a Great Job Last Semester?"

Group Leaders Training is a fast-paced, interactive, nut-and-bolts training event that all group leaders are required to attend whether they are new to group leadership or have led a group dozens of times. Some returning group leaders may resist having to come to training again, especially if their previous semester's experience was a good one. We simply explain that our pre-semester training is like spring training for a baseball team. Even the MVP from last year's World Series will be at spring training. He knows that you cannot cover the basics too often. And since our returning group leaders are the MVPs of our small groups system, we need them to be there every time.

While all of our Group Leaders Trainings have similar themes (see below), there are also fresh elements introduced each semester. These elements will be completely new to those who have attended before. Plus, every semester in the life of a church is different. So the vision for the coming semester will be fresh and exciting for repeaters as well. Our experience is that once you convince a seasoned leader to come to Group Leaders Training two or three times, he or she will see the value of it and make it a not-to-be-missed event.

The Specifics

Now that we've answered some of your questions about Group Leaders Training, let's see who is invited and what actually happens during those three hours:

Who

All group leaders (returning or new), coordinators who have already been identified and team leaders are required to attend the Group Leaders Training. But your RSVP list doesn't have to stop there. You might also invite those who are planning to host groups in their homes, even if they are not actually the coordinators or leaders. Really, there's probably no wrong person to invite to the training as long as they have a stake in making the next semester of groups a successful one.

Where

The most obvious location for Group Leaders Training is your church. But don't be afraid to spice it up a bit. If you think of a more fun place to hold the training, then hold it there. We once held Group Leaders Training in a conference room overlooking a local ice-skating rink. The unexpected venue brought a lot of energy to the meeting.

In general, hold your training in a location that is highly convenient for those attending. Don't make people drive a long way. You don't want to hand them ready-made excuses for why they can't be there. Also, don't get so creative that the venue hinders the effectiveness of the event. After all, the goal of the training is to train. Better to hold it at the church and have a high attendance than at a creative place across town that might hinder full participation. Be aware of the balance.

What

I (Nelson) still remember our first Journey Group Leaders Training. Because our services are held in rented facilities, we obviously couldn't host the training there. So we begged and borrowed a meeting space from a local church that was a little bit off the beaten path. We didn't need much room, because there were going to be fewer than 10 of us in attendance. I vividly remember that sinking feeling in my stomach as I wondered whether anyone would show up besides our paid staff. Well, they did. While I can't recall all that we talked about, I do remember that we huddled up some chairs, introduced ourselves and spent the next three hours brainstorming about how we could Fill and Facilitate the seven groups we were offering that fall. And, just like that, we were off and running with our new small groups systems.

Since that first time, the experience we provide at Group Leaders Training has expanded quite a bit. We still do the best we can to help old and new leaders Fill and Facilitate their groups, but we've also added lots of new elements. Instead of relying on one talking head for three hours, we've divided the training into multiple fast-paced segments. Pastors, other staff and team leaders all take part of the training. We also carve out time when group leaders meet with their team leaders for specific planning.

We like to take time to celebrate and reward those who attend. Sometimes that reward is tangible, like ice-cream gift certificates in the summer or Starbucks gift cards in the winter. Other times, it's a recognition from the stage for those who have served the most semesters as leaders. Think creatively and invite some converted party animals to help you plan the event. With a little forethought and a party planner's mindset, you can make your Group Leaders Training an effective, unforgettable extravaganza.

How

Creativity aside, here are the standard elements of a successful Group Leaders Training:

1. The basics (purpose of groups, filling group, following up on group signups)
2. Role clarification (responsibilities of a leader, coordinator and host)
3. Leading your group (using the covenant, leading your group in evangelism and service, handling pastoral care)
4. Training time (an original training element on leading a successful group)
5. Vision-casting (led by the lead pastor)

Let's examine each one in more detail.

The Basics

We teach "The Basics" at every Group Leaders Training. We may change how they are taught, or who teaches them, but the information on the purpose of groups, filling groups and following up on group sign-ups is presented. Just as the World Series MVP from the previous year will practice running, catching, hitting and throwing during spring training, your leaders need to be refreshed on the basic elements of a successful semester.

Purpose of Groups

When talking about the purpose of groups, we like to share a life-change story from the previous semester. We remind our leaders that what they are doing not only fits into the overall strategy of our church, but that they are also a key catalyst for life-change in the lives of those who participate.

Filling Groups

In our discussion on filling groups, we make sure that leaders understand how important it is to take personal responsibility for filling their groups. This is a great opportunity to create a sense of urgency in those whose groups aren't yet full. We try to help them fill their groups by scheduling them to work the groups information table at an upcoming service.

Following Up on Sign-Ups

Remind your leaders that you don't want anyone who signs up for a group to fall through the cracks. We often talk about how every person who signs up for a group is a person that matters. We affirm that no one signs up for a group without a prompting from God; so by following up, we are cooperating with God in His work in that person's life. Especially in a large church, it's easy for group sign-ups to look like numbers rather than individuals, so keep reminding your leaders about what's really going on here—a representation of the individual work of God in a person's life.

Role Clarification

Role clarification is particularly important for new group leaders. This is a very straightforward time where you talk through the three or four specific things that a leader and coordinator are expected to do (see Focus). Conclude this element of your training by inviting leaders and coordinators to sign and turn in their respective covenants. Make the signing of the covenant a serious time. If you take the expectations and commitment seriously, so will they.

Activate Principle

People take seriously the expectations that you take seriously.

On occasion, we have integrated role clarification and covenant signing into a short time of worship that concludes the Group Leaders Training. Sometimes we've had leaders turn in the covenant as they leave, as a final act of commitment. Other times, we have asked leaders to hand in the covenant during a time of communion, as they come forward to take the Lord's Supper. However you decide to communicate the importance of the leader and coordinator roles, make sure everyone leaves the training with a crystal-clear picture of what's expected of them. Clear roles will help ensure harmony during the facilitation of the upcoming groups semester.

Activate Principle

Agreements on the front end will prevent disagreements later.

Training Time

Training time is the heart of our three-hour event, providing the tools that every leader will need to head a successful group. Generally, these original talks are developed by our groups pastor to address key areas of facilitation. They can also be adapted from books and resources that teach leaders how to facilitate groups. Here are some examples of Journey training time talks:

- How to Lead a Group Without Talking So Much
- Building Community in Your Group
- Being a Shepherd to Your Group
- Including Others in the Conversation
- Handling the Disruptive Talkers and Other Personalities
- Raising Up New Group Leaders from Within
- The Three Types of People in Every Group (Unchurched, New Christians, Maturing)

You are not trying to cover all of these topics in one 30- to 45-minute session. Your goal, rather, is to cover all of the important points over the course of several semesters. The basics, role clarification, apprenticing and support from team leaders give most people enough insight and ability to facilitate a successful meeting. The training time, instead of being essential to effective Facilitation, is an additional tool that leaders can draw on to succeed. Take the opportunity to also highlight areas of key importance to your church and your groups system. (For downloads of previous group leader training talks, visit www.ActivateBook.com.)

Vision-casting

The vision-casting element of the training is a brief insider's look at what is happening over the next semester in our church. This time is best led by the senior pastor but can be delegated to another staff member on occasion. The vision-casting time is especially important if the upcoming semester is a church-wide campaign. Use this time to

1. Thank group leaders.
2. Share personal belief in the importance of groups.
3. Give an inside look into the next three months (sermon series topics, events, challenges or opportunities).
4. Share celebration stories from the previous semester (baptisms, increase in attendance, etc.).
5. Meet and pray for group leaders.

You may be tempted to spend too much time vision-casting. Like every other element of Group Leaders Training, this portion will need to be informative, fast-paced and carefully timed so that you can cover everything and keep everyone engaged.

With Regrets

What if a leader simply cannot attend the Group Leaders Training? Do the words "thirty lashes" and "public humiliation" mean anything to you? Okay, we are only joking, slightly. Seriously, do everything you can to continually raise the value of the training event and encourage leaders to attend.

Early on, we would let any excuse be sufficient for a group leader to miss training, but as we've come to believe more and more in the power of groups, we will now often give a little push back to someone who says they can't make it. We'll gently ask why and wait for a response. Sometimes, just asking why is enough to convince someone to change her schedule. Other times, after hearing an excuse, we'll simply ask the leader if he or she can rearrange his or her plans to be at the training. We've asked people to reschedule dentist appointments, hair appointments and even business flights so that they can attend. It's amazing how flexible people will become when you are firm and clear about the importance of the event. We can do this with all sincerity, because we truly believe that Group Leaders Training is that valuable.

Still, even with all of your powers of persuasion, sometimes a group leader simply won't be able to make the training. So what do you do? To begin with, make sure that they listen to the entire training on CD or MP3 after the fact and then schedule a one-on-one meeting with their team leader to discuss all of the information that was covered. Have them sign the covenant in front of their team leader at this meeting. Beyond that, you could hold a mini-training if there are a handful of leaders who can't make it. The key is to be understanding of their absence but clear that you take their leadership of a group very seriously.

Facilitate Principle #2: Structuring the First Group Meeting

We all know the power of a first impression. The first group meeting is a major first impression for people who have never been in groups before. And for those who know how groups work, the first meeting sets the tone for how this particular semester will go. A strong first meeting is the foundation for a successful semester. To get everyone on the same page and primed for a great semester, there are a few key things the group leader must discuss. Like the overall small groups system, these things are simple but need to be examined and understood thoroughly to be effective. The three most important items to focus on in the first meeting are (1) the group covenant, (2) key dates, and (3) the importance of time. Let's discuss each one.

The Group Covenant
A lot will happen in that first meeting—introductions, prayer, an overview of the curriculum, snacking/socializing, and more. But the most important thing that should happen is a detailed discussion of the group

covenant. Because of the covenant's importance, we advise leaders to allow at least 15 minutes to go over it with their group members. The primary purpose of the covenant is to call each member to a higher level of spiritual growth.

Activate Principle
The group covenant is ultimately a
spiritual growth tool.

A good covenant fulfills both of these activate principles. In addition, the covenant allows for smooth facilitation of the group and, in the event of a problem, provides common ground for handling difficult people. If you make the covenant a priority, so will group leaders and group members. On the following page is a copy of the group covenant we use (for an electronic copy, visit www.ActivateBook.com).

The group leader should be ready to walk the members through the covenant and answer any questions. We encourage our leaders to read the covenant line by line and offer commentary when necessary. Some leaders may feel slightly uncomfortable doing this at first, but as we reinforce in Group Leader Training, the clearer they are about the covenant, the fewer problems they will have in their group. We've found that once group leaders understand how the covenant will help them facilitate their group in the most life-transforming way, they start presenting it boldly.

Activate Principle
People grow best when the accountability is high
and the expectations are clear.

The Journey

Growth Group Covenant

Welcome to Growth Groups at The Journey. Congratulations on your desire to grow deeper in your relationship with God through this weekly study and the relationships that will begin in this Growth Group.

As a member of this group, you will be asked to enter into a covenant with the other members to make this Growth Group a priority. To be a part of the group, you are asked to make the following commitments:

1. I will make this group a priority by attending each week, keeping up with my assignments and participating openly in group discussion.

2. I will regularly attend The Journey services and contribute to the ministry of the church through my attendance, giving, service, and inviting of others.

3. I will strive to build authentic relationships with those in this group by showing care, providing encouragement and praying for their needs.

4. I will serve together with my group once a month during the semester and will *play* together with my group at least once.

5. I will explore honestly my next steps for spiritual growth.

_____   _____
Name   Date

Three of the Most Common Questions

Once the leader presents the covenant, he or she should allow for questions. Many times there will be no questions at all and people will sign the covenant right on the spot. However, more than likely there will be a few basic clarifications and perhaps one or two serious questions.

1. Do I Have to Attend Worship Services to Be in a Growth Group?

This comes from the second statement in the covenant where we ask group members to "attend, give, serve and invite" as part of the growth-group experience. The short answer is, "Yes, as much as possible." The leader should remind everyone that groups are not meant to be stand-alone stations of spiritual growth, but are part of the overall commitment to being a fully engaged member of our church. Often, the person asking this question is a member or regular attender of another church, who found out about our growth groups and wanted to take part. Our philosophy is that someone who has another home church should not be a part of groups at The Journey. In fact, we do not allow someone who is an active member at another church to participate in our groups. If this situation arises, tell your leaders to explain the philosophy gracefully, in a conversation after the group wraps up.

Recently, I (Nelson) had to explain to someone from another prominent church in our area that they couldn't participate in our groups, because we require Sunday attendance as part of the commitment. At first, this person was a bit perturbed. I went on to explain that we encourage people to attend a group at their own church and to be fully engaged there. He left our meeting somewhat frustrated, but I knew it was the right decision for everyone involved. About two months later, I received an email from this person thanking me for, in his words, "returning [him] back to [his] flock." He had recommitted himself to engaging within his church and was now growing more than ever. If you do not allow people from other churches to join your groups, that word will get out among other churches and over time it will be less of an issue. Not to mention that other local pastors will thank you!

Some people think that our mindset on this issue goes against the Kingdom mentality that all churches are on the same team. Not at all. We believe that encouraging someone to keep the commitments they have made to their own church is one of the most beneficial things we can do for God's kingdom. Every church needs its own fully committed people as we work together to build up the kingdom of God.

You might have someone attend your group who has never been to a Sunday service and is uncertain about signing the covenant and making that commitment. Again, reiterate how important the Sunday service is and challenge the person to give it a shot over the 10 to 12 weeks that the group will meet. Ask the person to use this time to commit to checking out the church. He or she may not attend every Sunday throughout the semester, but simply showing up is an important first step for someone who was not attending at all.

2. Do I Have to Commit to Attend Every Week if I Sign the Covenant?

This question often comes from the first statement in the covenant. We usually answer with a smile, "If you love the Lord, you'll be here every week." And then we go on to explain that the tenet actually states that you will make group attendance a priority. This means that you will attend group every time it is at all possible. We then assure the person that everyone has to miss from time to time due to a sick child, last-minute work responsibilities, etc., but the commitment is to make his or her presence a priority. We encourage the person to contact a leader and also keep up with the reading if they do have to miss a meeting.

3. Do I Have to Sign the Covenant to Attend the Group?

Again, the short answer to this question is "Yes," but you may want to dig a little deeper and find the root of this question. You might simply ask, "What do you mean?" and let the person further explain. Often the question behind the question is about particular parts of the covenant that can be clarified easily, or it may be a misunderstanding of why the covenant is necessary.

In my second semester of leading a group, I (Nelson) was asked this question by a young lady in our group. She was adamant that she couldn't sign the covenant, but she wanted to attend the group. I kept asking her to explain, and finally discovered that her hang-up was on the word "covenant." Because English was her second language, she was interpreting the word to mean either a legal contract or a covenant with God that would bring about serious consequences (think Old Testament punishment). I assured her that it was neither. Rather, the covenant was an agreement we were making with the other members of the group, and that it was a standard operating agreement that should be taken seriously but would not result in legal action or Old Testament retribution! When she understood, she signed gladly and ended up being a very active member of the group.

Look for the question behind every question. Find out where the questioning person is coming from. Keep asking, "What do you mean?" or "What can I clarify for you?" until the real issue rises to the top. Then graciously, but without compromising the strong intent of the covenant, answer the question as honestly as possible. We've found that calling people to a high standard with the group covenant not only ensures a successful semester but also may be the best thing you can do for their spiritual growth.

Recently, I (Nelson) received a strong covenant reaction from a new group member. He was extremely resistant to the covenant's ideals. We decided to talk after the meeting and the man informed me that he had "never been to church that much." The more we talked, the more I sensed that he wasn't even a follower of Jesus. He asked if he couldn't "just take it easy and attend from time to time" since he held a high-level corporate job and was so new to the church. I told him that he could attend our worship services as often or as infrequently as he'd like, but that the commitments of the covenant were firm. After some initial uncertainty, he agreed to give it a try. He became a regular group attender. He started coming to service every week. Shortly after the semester ended, he gave his life to Jesus. At his baptism, he thanked me and the church for the accountability the group provided to him in his spiritual journey. Again, the covenant is primarily a spiritual growth document.

Signing and Collecting the Covenant

Once the leader has discussed the covenant, he or she should give everyone a chance to sign and turn in his or her copy. If someone asks to take it home to think about and bring it back the next week, that's okay—just make sure it comes back. The group leader should keep the covenants together in a safe place until the semester is over. There's no need for them to go on file at the church, as they are commitments made between group members for only that one semester.

For the first meeting, leaders should plan to make two copies of the covenant for everyone in the group—one for them to sign and turn in and another copy to keep. Giving them a copy to take home is an important step that underscores the significance of what they have just signed. While two simple copies work fine, you can be more creative with the one they take home, if you like. Some artistic group leaders have made more formal copies of the covenant and given them to each person.

One leader we know of made a huge covenant, had everyone sign it and then displayed it at every meeting. Our favorite idea is to give an oversized bookmark with key dates on one side and the covenant on the other. How you decide to do it doesn't really matter. What matters is making sure that every group participant can keep a copy of the covenant, which will reinforce its magnitude and provide for smoother group facilitation.

When Someone Violates the Covenant

The covenant is primarily a spiritual growth tool, but it can also be used as a foundation when dealing with problems. Confrontation rarely happens. But when it does, the covenant plays a big role.

One time at The Journey, a group leader found that a member of his group was sharing personal information (discussed in the group) about another member with other people in the church, in an unhealthy way. It was gossip at best; character assassination at worst. The leader asked the slanderer to meet with him after the next week's group meeting. In a soft but direct way the leader asked if the accusation was true. The group member affirmed that it was. The group leader then said something to the effect, "On the first day of this group, we all signed a covenant stating that we would 'strive to build authentic relationships' and that personal information shared in the group context was outside of the intent of this statement. Are you willing to stop spreading this information and to ask the person harmed for forgiveness? If not, I'm going to have to ask you to leave our group." While the messy relational damage had already been done, the covenant created an avenue for the situation to be repaired.

Other times, we've been able to refer back to the covenant when talking privately with someone about his or her Sunday attendance, the issue of dominating group discussion or harboring an uncooperative spirit. We have been called to hold our people accountable, and this tool helps immensely. Of course, the covenant does not solve all of the problems that will arise in a group, but it does give a common foundation of agreement on which harmony can be established and maintained.

The Syllabus

The syllabus is the second most important handout, which naturally leads to the second most important discussion of the night. For the semesters when the leaders choose curriculum, every group leader must prepare and submit a syllabus for approval before the semester begins. During the fall semester, when we do a church-wide campaign, we prepare the standardized syllabus for leaders to distribute to group members.

You are probably familiar with what a standard syllabus looks like, since you came through the educational system. As you might expect, the syllabus is simply a list of key dates for the upcoming group along with the reading/study assignments for each week the group will meet. Even if a group doesn't have outside reading, a syllabus lets everyone know the meeting dates and what topics will be discussed on those days.

While the syllabus is helpful to group members, the main reason we have each leader prepare one is for their own benefit. The exercise forces the group leader to think through the semester, organize the curriculum and plan all of the key dates well in advance of the first group meeting. If a leader is unable to prepare a simple syllabus for the upcoming semester, it's a good indication that person is not ready to lead.

At the first meting, the leader should walk through the syllabus and encourage everyone to transfer the key dates from the syllabus to his or her personal calendar. These will most likely include:

- When the group will be off (no meeting)
- When the group will meet at a different location
- When the group will do an evangelism outreach together
- When the group will do something fun together
- When the group will serve at the worship services
- Date of the last group meeting

Of course, these dates will have to be reiterated throughout the semester, but taking a few moments to ask everyone to add them to their schedule will build excitement about all that is to come. For a sample syllabus, visit www.ActivateBook.com.

Staying On Time

The first group meeting, and every meeting to follow, should be 90 minutes or less. The group leader absolutely has to keep the meeting from dragging on beyond the time limit. Many people who show up for the first meeting with uncertainties about small groups in general will feel a lot better if the first meeting stays on topic and wraps up on time. If a question about the covenant or syllabus drags on too long, the leader can offer to meet with the individual after the group is dismissed. Be respectful of everyone's time. Here's a sample first meeting agenda that we provide to our group leaders:

Possible Itinerary for the First Growth-Group Meeting

1. Allow people to arrive, talk, and snack (15 min.).

2. Pray (1 min.).

3. Have participants introduce themselves and share what they do, where they live and why they decided to join the group (10 min.).

4. Introductory game. Have everyone tell three things about themselves, two being true and one being false. Have everyone else try to guess which one is false. Any other interactive game (10 min.).

5. Introduce the group study briefly. Hand out Growth Group syllabus and any other important information. Answer any questions and cover key dates (15 min.).

6. Hand out the Growth Group Covenant. Read through the Growth Group Covenant carefully with the group. Explain the points as you read each one. Answer any questions. If anyone tries to be difficult and disagreeable, offer to talk with him or her individually at the end of the meeting (5 to 15 min.).

7. Explain and ask for volunteers for the different roles within the group: Play Coordinator, Food Coordinator, etc. (5 min.).

8. Share prayer requests and pray together (10 min.).

9. Talk and eat (15 minutes).

When Someone Misses the First Meeting

Someone will miss the first meeting. It's inevitable. New people may join after the group begins. When this happens, we encourage group leaders to hold a quick meeting with new people right after the next group meeting to discuss/sign the covenant and go over key dates. Generally, this can be done in 10 to 15 minutes. The most important thing is to make sure that all new members understand and sign the covenant.

Use the first meeting to set the tone, disseminate information, get to know each other and have fun! What you do during these 90 minutes will go a long way toward ensuring proper facilitation of the group throughout the rest of the semester.

Facilitate Principle #3: Conducting Week-to-Week Facilitation

Group leaders and coordinators are primarily responsible for the week-to-week facilitation of groups. Their key responsibilities are to:

1. Provide a reminder about the meeting each week via a phone call, an email or a text message, depending on the group. In this communication, the leader or coordinator will remind the group of the week's assignment and any important dates. This can be brief, but should be done about two days before the group meets each and every week.

2. Follow up with those who unexpectedly miss the meeting. Just check in and see if everything is okay. This will help people feel connected even if they miss a week or two. Those who contact the leader about their absence before the group may not require follow-up unless the leader feels like he or she should check in (e.g., if the person had to miss for a medical reason or because of an important meeting and the group was praying for that person).

3. Send out the group's prayer requests after each meeting.

We like to keep the week-to-week facilitation responsibilities to a minimum. Are you surprised that "submit a weekly attendance report" is not on our list? We have found that such a report is simply not that helpful to us and is often an unnecessary burden on the group leaders. Since the group leader is already following up on the people who miss the group meeting, what practical purpose does a weekly attendance report serve? You might say, "Well, we take attendance each Sunday, so why not in our groups?" That's a great point. We do believe that worship service attendance is very important as one measure of overall church health and for strategic reasons like starting an additional service or planning seasonal events. The same thinking does not apply to week-to-week attendance with groups. They're a different animal. They operate on the basis of tightly assigned relationships. These attendance numbers are not as important as the year-to-year trends for worship services.

Two Questions

We have found that all we need is an average attendance in the groups number at least once a semester in order to pinpoint the ratio between group sign-ups and group show-ups. In our experience, the best approach to attendance is to ask all group leaders to answer two questions near the end of the semester:

Question #1
How many people signed up for your group that never showed up?
This gives a ratio of sign-ups to show-ups, which is crucial for projecting how many groups you'll need in your next semester. It also lets you know how well you are doing with filling your groups. Your goal is to keep this ratio as low as possible. But almost every group will have some percentage of people who sign up but never show up. If the gap starts to

get too wide, you may want to ask if someone is falling through the cracks in your Fill process. If the gap gets too small, you may want to ask if you are doing enough to recruit "nominal attenders" to join groups. Only your core will consistently sign up and show up.

Your sign-ups to show-ups ratio will also let you know when you need to close a group. For example, if your goal is to have 15 active members in each group and the ratio between sign-ups and show-ups is 20 percent, you will probably want to close a group when it hits 20 to 22 people (since four will probably never show up and one or two will drop out early on) so that each group will start with 15 to 16 people. Remember, it's always better for a group to be slightly over-attended than under-attended. See "Facilitation and Group Leader Retention."

Question #2
On a good night, how many people show up for your group?
This is a useful question. The response will be based on a group's good/ average night, instead of week to week when attendance fluctuates due to weather, miscommunication, vacations, etc. The number you get will tell you how many people in your church are actually involved in groups. It will give you a sense of the health of your overall system. In a strong system, this number will closely resemble adult attendance at the worship services. In fact, here's a challenge: Make it a goal for your weekly group attendance to match your weekly adult worship service attendance.

Let these two questions help you gauge the health of your system and plan for your next semester!

Week-to-Week Pastoral Care
Group leaders are in the perfect position to provide pastoral care for their own group. They will have greater knowledge of what's going on in the group than anyone else in the church and can lead their group

members to care for one another. If someone is in the hospital, that person's group leader should head the charge to support him or her and his or her family. If someone is having a difficult time financially, the group leader should lead the group to meet those needs. If we empower our group leaders to step up to this role, pastoral care will be done more quickly and more efficiently. If an issue arises that the group leader can't handle, then he or she can bring in her team leader or the groups pastor for help and support.

Prayer is one element of pastoral care that all group members provide to one another. At the end of every group meeting, the leader should set aside 10 minutes to share prayer requests and pray. The leader or coordinator should write down these prayer requests as they are being shared and email them to everyone in the group the next day. That way, all of the group's members can be praying for one another throughout the week.

Week-to-Week Communication from the Groups Pastor

An important part of week-to-week facilitation is the weekly communication from the groups pastor to each group leader, generally in the form of an email at the start of each week. In this email, the groups pastor will highlight specific issues related to successful facilitation, and communicate any last-minute notes to the group leaders (like the special once-a-semester events). This is a weekly occurrence, so make sure you have a sustainable process in place to ensure that the communications are on time and helpful. Here's a process you can adapt for your church.

1. *The groups pastor drafts the email on Thursday* (to be sent the following Monday). The email should include the following elements:

- A leadership/facilitation tip. We call this "just in time" or "ongoing" training. The tip might be on how to lead an icebreaker game, how to identify potential leaders in your group or how to deal with questions you don't know the answers to.

- Information on upcoming events like baptisms, church events, membership classes. Remind them to share these with their group.

- A reminder about the teaching topic for the upcoming Sunday.

2. *The email is sent to all group leaders on Monday morning.* All of your leaders should be expecting this and should let you know if they don't receive it.

3. *The groups pastor follows up with any replies to the email throughout the week and drafts the next week's email on Thursday.* These weekly emails become easier to do the longer you do them. And we've found that our group leaders love and rely on them. Here is a sample of a group leaders' update that was sent right before the summer groups kicked off:

GG Theme of the Week:
Take the initiative to *ask* people to join your group.

1. ASK people you see or meet at church on Sunday if they have joined a group yet. If they say no, then ask them to join yours.

2. ASK friends you know from previous Growth Groups (who haven't joined a group yet) to join your group.

3. ASK one person whom you know (from your work, your school, your apartment building, and so forth.), and who does not go to church anywhere, to join your Growth Group this semester.

Memory Verse of the Week:

" 'For I know the plans that I have for you,' declares the LORD, 'plans to prosper you and not to harm you. Plans to give you hope and a future'" (Jer. 29:11, *NIV*).

Important GG Info:

1. Follow up with every person who has signed up for your Growth Group and who will be signing up in the coming days. Every person is important, so don't let anyone slip through the cracks!

2. Take time to hand out and explain the Growth Group Covenant at your first group meeting this week. Have everyone who intends on being a part of your group sign the covenant and hand it in to you. The covenants are for you to keep.

3. Not everyone who has signed up for your Growth Group will show up the first week. That's okay. Just be sure to follow up with those who are absent the very next day, and let them know that they were missed. Encourage them to join the group next week.

4. Also, remember the two Coordinator emails that need to be sent. One, the day after your first meeting, the Prayer Requests need to be emailed to every member of the group. Two, a reminder email needs to be sent to everyone a day or two before the next group meeting reminding them of the upcoming meeting.

Thanks again for serving. We're praying for you this week as your group begins. Let us know how it goes!

Serving with you . . .
Pastor Kerrick

P.S.—Remember, this Sunday "God on Film" gets rolling as we have fun exploring *The Hitchhiker's Guide: What Is the Purpose of Life?* Invite a friend to join you as we tackle this difficult question. See you on Sunday!

Here's a weekly update that was sent near the end of a fall semester.

GG Tip of the Week:
Motivate my group to multiply.

As a Growth Group Leader/Coordinator you play an important role in making sure we have plenty of Growth Groups for everyone to get plugged into next semester. You are also helping new group leaders take an important step of growth in their own lives. You do this by identifying those in your group with the ability to lead and encourage them to take this important step in their lives. So, think about your current group and let me know the answer to the following two questions:

1. *Will I lead a Spring 2008 Growth Group?* Spring 2008 Growth Groups begin the week of February 11 and last through May 3. Spring Growth Groups are fun because you get to choose what kind of Growth Group you want to lead (e.g., topic/book/video/type/location).

2. *Who from my current group would make a good leader?* Identify one person, or more, from your group who you think could

lead a group next semester. Just email me or pass their name along to your team leader.

I've attached a list of approved curriculum for you to look at!

GG Important Information:

The Discussion Questions for this week (week 8) are posted on our website. The link is: http://www.journeymetro.com/resources/ntc.

- Email your group today to remind them you are meeting this week since you had last week off.

- You should have received an invite from Pastor Nelson inviting you to a special Journey Christmas Party for Leaders. It is December 16th from 2:30 to 3:30 P.M. at the Manhattan Center immediately following the 1:00 P.M. service. Let me know if you have any questions . . . you can RSVP by replying to this email.

- FYI . . . In our Growth Groups next week we are asking that you take a few minutes to share about The Journey's Embracing My City special offering (week of December 2). On Thursday I will be emailing you information about EMC to cover in your group next week, so be on the lookout for it.

Thanks again for everything you do. It is very important that you get an answer to your team leader from the two questions above (ASAP) so that we will be able to provide groups for everyone at The Journey! Let me know if there is anything that I can do to help with this.

Praying for you this week . . .
Adam

P.S.—This Sunday we wrap up our New Testament Challenge series in Manhattan with "The Challenge of Eternity," and in Jersey City we will be talking about "The Challenge of Obedience." See you there!

http://www.journeymetro.com

For more examples, visit www.ActivateBook.com.

Facilitate Principle #4: Conducting Monthly Facilitation

Team leaders and group leaders work together on monthly facilitation. As we mentioned earlier, group leaders should meet with their team leaders at least once during the semester to discuss how the groups are going and to talk through any issues that may have surfaced. We call this meeting the Growth Group Huddle.

The Growth Group Huddle

During the huddle, the team leader should encourage the group leaders, promote the groups system by being aware of new potential team leaders among them, gather feedback on the semester and pray with everyone. The huddle can happen over dinner or in a short meeting following a Sunday service. If you aren't yet to the point of having team leaders, you and your staff should run the huddle with all of your group leaders.

Your role as a leader of the groups system is to ensure that these meetings are taking place and to debrief with the team leaders after the fact. Even though these huddles are short, they provide invaluable feedback for making your small groups system more effective the following semester. Here is a format for the huddle we provide our team leaders:

Team Leader Huddle Guide

ASK everyone to share something good/positive that has happened in their life or in their group in the last few weeks. *It's
easy to be negative and to talk about the frustrations. Begin by finding
things to be thankful for.*

ASK how the individual groups are going. Are there groups
that are thriving? Do some groups need help or additional
leadership? *Remind your Group Leaders/Coordinators to be diligent
about leading their groups to serve.*

ASK each leader who they have identified as possible future
leaders. Encourage them to give those people responsibility in
the group. *Be sure that every group has asked someone to serve as a
Coordinator. Securing Coordinators and asking for possible future
leaders NOW will make the process of forming groups for the next semester easier later on.*

ASK if there is anything you can do for them or if there is a
specific way that you can be praying for them. Say thank you.
Pray. *Remind them that you pray for them daily and want to serve
them in any way that you can.*

FOLLOW UP with your Coach after every GG Huddle. Keep
your Coach updated and let him or her know how he or she
can help and serve you.

Facilitate Principle #5:
Conducting Semester Facilitation

Once a semester, you will need to address important areas of facilitation, based on the overall structure of your groups system. These might include evangelism projects, serving at the worship services, promoting baptism or membership, or planning a fun event for the group.

Feel free to add your own semester expectations to your group, but remember to keep the focus simple. Asking your groups to do too many outside activities will distract from the week-to-week experience. At The Journey, we try to limit our focus to no more than four expectations—and only one or two that require you to miss a weekly group meeting. Let's look at four of these in detail.

Evangelism Projects

We believe that it's important for groups to be involved in a planned evangelism project once a semester, either in place of or in addition to the weekly group meeting. Our most effective group evangelism project is always Servant Evangelism (SE), where groups do an outreach to people in the area where they meet. We plan these outreaches strategically so that they'll occur just before a big day at The Journey. (For a free resource on Servant Evangelism, visit www.ActivateBook.com.)

Group members often tell us that doing an SE outreach was one of their most memorable experiences from the semester. Not only do these outreaches bring your group closer together, but they also push group members out of their comfort zones. Perhaps most important, they keep the group from becoming inwardly focused. As you lead groups to pray for unchurched people in the weeks leading up to SE and encourage them during the outreach, they have a renewed sense of evangelism toward those around them. Build a semester evangelism project into the DNA of your groups from the very beginning. You'll see huge rewards.

Serving Together at the Worship Services

Asking your groups to serve together at the worship service at least once a semester is a great way to integrate groups into the complete life of the church. You can consider asking groups to serve no matter how many you have, but this will work especially well for churches with more than 20 groups. You'll be giving your groups an opportunity to invest in the worship experience by serving in key volunteer positions, which will spark a feeling of responsibility toward the church. As you know, relationships (small groups) and responsibility (serving) are two of the most important factors for assimilation. So how does the serving work?

1. Identify the areas in your church where people with limited training can simply show up and serve. At The Journey this means serving as a greeter, at the refreshments table, on the pre-service prayer team or as an usher.

2. Assign each group to a worship service and give them a set time to show up for a brief training. We ask them to be there an hour before the service starts.

3. When the group arrives, do the brief training and assign people to specific roles.

4. Debrief after the service and ask how you could improve the experience.

5. Encourage the groups who serve to share a meal after the service.

6. Use this service opportunity as a way to sign up people to be regular servers.

Keeping your groups connected to the worship service can provide great synergy, and it's a perfect way to raise up new volunteers.

Promoting Baptism and Membership

At least once during the semester, ask group leaders to take a few minutes to discuss the importance of baptism and membership. This doesn't have to be a full theological discussion; you simply want them to bring the issues to the forefront. At The Journey, we strategically plan for this to happen a few weeks before the next baptism or membership class. We may ask leaders to have someone in their group share a baptism experience and then have people who need to be baptized sign up. And when someone in a group decides to be baptized, we encourage the entire growth group to attend the ceremony and support them.

We may ask the leader to share about church membership and encourage everyone in the group who is not a member to attend the class together. We have learned over the years that "ownership precedes membership." Once someone is thriving and serving in a group, membership is a natural step. You can also use your weekly emails as a chance to remind leaders to talk about baptism and membership. Don't be hesitant. These are important spiritual growth components. You should be asking your leaders to highlight them.

Planning a Fun Event

Each semester, encourage your group to play together at least one time. They can plan anything from attending a sporting event, going out for dinner, taking in a movie or going bowling. Let each group decide what they want to do. Leaders should schedule the event for about halfway through the semester. They may even consider having everyone invite their spouse/significant other.

Activate Principle
The group that plays together grows together!

You can build this play night, which will ideally replace the meeting time one week, into the syllabus from the very beginning. Keeping the fun consistent with your group's meeting time will allow more people to take part. However, if everyone in the group agrees, there is certainly nothing wrong with doing your fun event any other time. Here are a few keys to a successful fun event:

1. Appoint a leader for the fun event, preferably someone besides the group leader.

2. Plan an event that everyone can participate in without prior experience. Dinner and a movie will attract more participation than a rock-climbing day (unless everyone in the group is a rock climber!).

3. Keep the participation commitment as low as possible. A night out will attract greater participation than an overnight retreat.

4. Keep the cost low.

5. Make sure there will be plenty of time and opportunity to talk and build relationships. After all, that's the point!

Easter and the Spring Semester

For most churches, Easter is the biggest day of the year. Rightly so, since it is a celebration of the resurrection of Jesus Christ—the most significant event in history! Because Easter is such a big day, and because it falls during your spring groups semester, it gets some extra attention when planning your spring calendar.

The week leading up to Easter should be given priority on all of your spring groups' syllabi. Some churches choose to give groups the week between Palm Sunday and Easter Sunday off. Think of it as spring break for your groups. You can encourage people to use the time off to reach out to their unchurched neighbors and invite their friends to attend Easter services with them. At the same time, ask all of your groups to participate in a day of fasting leading up to Easter, as they consider whom to invite. The groups pastor may want to provide a short study sheet or mini-curriculum that group leaders can introduce a week or two before Easter to help their group members know how to give priority to the opportunities that Easter presents. At The Journey, Easter usually gets a special outreach as well. All of our groups are encouraged to participate in a Servant Evangelism project. We've also done simple prayer walks through the neighborhoods around the church.

Activate Principle

Maximize the groups' experience leading up to Easter to ensure that Easter is indeed the celebration it should be!

Groups and Other Special Events

From time to time, you may need to focus a week or two of small groups meetings on an important current issue or event in the church. For example, if there's a big special offering going on, or the kick-off of a capital campaign, you may ask your group leaders to preempt a meeting or two to discuss it. While such "positive interruptions" shouldn't happen every semester, it's perfectly reasonable to focus on a special emphasis like this once a year or every couple of years. As with Easter, you may want to give your group leaders a special curriculum they can use to facilitate discussion and prayer around what's going on.

A short break in the curriculum can help your groups' facilitation. It provides a mini-release for the group—a pleasant distraction from the norm. The key to making these variations work is advanced planning.

As you prepare for the upcoming semester, think about the overall direction of the church. Will any big events or big issues fall during the semester? If so, how do you want to address them in your groups?

Facilitation and Group Leader Retention

Your semester will be successfully facilitated when you have provided environments for group member life-change, through the power of the Holy Spirit, and have given your group leaders a positive experience. Ensuring that your group leaders will want to lead again and again is one of the major reasons to focus on facilitation. They need to know that you are there to support them. They need to feel blessed and ministered to at the end of a semester. We believe that the key measurement of a small groups system's health is leader retention. When it's all said and done, do your leaders want to do it again?

Activate Principle

If you take care of your group leaders, they will take care of your small groups system.

At the end of each Facilitation month, take the time to debrief with your leaders. Find out how you could make their job easier, more impacting or more effective. Take the lessons they teach you and incorporate them into your planning for the next semester. Do all you can to see that those who you want to lead again do in fact lead again. And don't forget to celebrate with all of your leaders when the semester is finished! Then, take a deep breath, and Focus.

By following the simple Activate system of Focus, Form, Fill and Facilitate, you can develop a small groups ministry that, though detailed, isn't complicated. It is a system that operates without hiring dozens of staff people, that regularly sees 100 percent adult participation, that provides a place where life-change consistently happens, and that you, your staff and your volunteers are passionate about.

We hope this conversation will continue as you begin to take action on the practices and principles you've just studied. Our goal for The Journey and for your church is to see the power of God's Spirit work in and through us, and the people we shepherd, at the highest level possible. To that end, we continue to improve and innovate our small groups system week after week. Since we are all on this journey together, we want to be able to continue sharing with you as you share with us.

To help facilitate our ongoing conversation, we have set up a website containing a plethora of both the tools we've mentioned in this book and many that have not been discussed. One extremely valuable tool that we simply did not have the space to include in these pages is a sample calendar of *everything* that happens week to week in a year of the Activate small groups system. We believe this calendar will help you tie the entire system together for your church. You will find the calendar—and much more—when you visit: www.ActivateBook.com.

We look forward to hearing your stories of small-group success. Thank you for investing in *Activate* for yourself, for your team and for all of your future fully developing followers of Christ.

Your partners in ministry,

Nelson and Kerrick